Bonnie Prince Charlie & the Highland Army in Derby

In Memory of my Beloved Wife Sue
1947 – 2012

Prince Charles Edward Stuart at about the age
of 13 in 1735, after the original in the National
Portrait Gallery attributed to Nicolas de
Largillière.

Bonnie Prince Charlie & the Highland Army in Derby

Brian Stone

Scarthin Books
Cromford, Derbyshire
2015

ISBN 9781900446167

Published by

Scarthin Books, Scarthin, Cromford,
Derbyshire DE4 3QF

nickscarthin@gmail.com
www.scarthinbooks.com
01629 823272

Contents

Illustrations

Frontispiece: Bonnie Prince Charlie at about the age of 13 in 1735 (author's collection)

After page 102:

1. Cowley's Map of Derbyshire, 1744

2. King James III, the "Old Pretender", father of Bonnie Prince Charlie (author's collection)

3. Bonnie Prince Charlie as a child, c.1737 (author's collection)

4. Plan of the Highland Army that marched to Derby, by Lord Elcho (author's collection)

5. A highland "targe" (shield) left behind at Bradley Hall by the Highland Army in 1745

6. The mortar left behind at Derby by the Jacobite Army on their retreat, now at Kedleston Hall

7. The notice attached to the mortar giving details of its provenance.

8. The Meynell town house, Derby, requisitioned for Lord Pitsligo

9. Bingham's House, Derby, requisitioned for Lord Nairne

10. the George Inn, Derby (now Mr. Jorrocks pub), where the Duke of Devonshire raised the Derbyshire Blues regiment

11. Plaque at the Mr. Jorrocks Pub commemorating the Duke's raising

12. Swarkestone Bridge, the furthest point reached by the rebel army

13. The Cairn at Swarkestone, marking the furthest point south

14. The Bonnie Prince Charlie statue, Full street, Derby, adjacent to where Exeter House once stood

15. The Bonnie Prince Charlie Room, Derby Museum, with panelling rescued from Exeter House

16. Exeter House, Derby, demolished in 1854 (author's collection)

17. Plaque in Derby Cathedral commemorating the service held by the Jacobites on 5th. December, 1745

Illustrations, *continued*

Photographs of houses and monuments, etc. are by the author.

Maps in the Text

Preface

On a summer's day, in July 1745, amidst gale force winds and heavy rain, a sprightly young man set foot on the cropped turf of Eriskay, a tiny island in the Outer Hebrides of Scotland. His name was Charles Edward Stuart, he was aged just 24 and he had come to regain his father's throne. He had with him seven loyal companions, several of them septuagenarians, a large sum of money in gold and a small quantity of swords and muskets. With these slender resources few could have foreseen that within less than five months he would have raised an army of highland clansmen, seized the capital of Scotland, soundly beaten a government army at Prestonpans and invaded England, reaching the quiet little town of Derby on 4th December, only 120 miles short of London.

This book examines this extraordinary sequence of events, perhaps the most serious and unpredictable threat that the Hanoverian government of Britain had ever faced; in particular, it looks in detail at the decisions that took the Jacobite army to Derby, the reasons why they decided to retreat from there back to Scotland, and the impact that their invasion had on the town of Derby and the county of Derbyshire

There has been a previous work on the Jacobite Rebellion in Derbyshire - L Eardley- Simpson's book "Derby and the Forty-five" published in 1933. It is now more than 80 years old, and modern historical scholarship had covered much ground and uncovered much illuminating detail since then that was not available to him. There has been a resurgence of interest in Jacobite studies in the past twenty years which has produced much ground-breaking material, in particular, Paul Kleber Monod's "Jacobitism and the English People", Dr Eveline Cruickshanks' "Political Untouchables - the Tories and the '45", F J McLynn's "The Jacobite Army in England 1745" and Dr Jonathan Oates' "The Jacobite Invasion of 1745 in North West England". In addition, there are many aspects of his book with which one is tempted profoundly to disagree - on the nature and extent of Jacobite support and sympathy in the county, the Prince's prospects of success and the reasons for the fateful decision on 5th December to return to Scotland. It seemed to me, therefore, that the time was ripe for a reassessment of these events in the light of current historical knowledge. It also gives me an opportunity of correcting some of the book's short-comings (not least its inadequate and badly presented bibliography) and of putting a different and, I believe, more accurate interpretation on the events that Simpson analyses.

Major Eardley-Simpson was a well-known and highly respected member of the legal profession in Derby and was a partner in the firm of solicitors that still bears his name, Taylor Simpson and Mosley. However, he was also a convinced Jacobite, an adherent of the Stuart succession, and a member of the Jacobite "Order of the White Rose". Some years ago, while giving a talk on Derbyshire in the Jacobite Rebellion to a local society, I happened to meet a very elderly surveyor who had known Eardley-Simpson well; he told me that his Jacobitism was so entrenched that he refused to rise and drink the monarch's health at Law Society dinners, so it is clear that when he wrote the book he had an agenda - it has a strong pro-Jacobite slant which, in my opinion, gives a partisan and misleading impression of what occurred in Derbyshire in 1745.

Having said that, there is no denying the value of his work in making accessible, for the first time, the astonishing story of the Jacobite invasion of Derbyshire, the occupation of Derby by the Gaelic-speaking clansmen of Bonnie Prince Charlie's army, and the decision to retreat to Scotland taken at the Council of War on 5th December, arguably one of the great turning-points of 18th Century British history. This book owes him an enormous debt of gratitude for his pioneering work, and my task in writing it would have been infinitely more difficult without the invaluable research that he carried out in the local and national archives. I have tried to supplement his efforts with modern scholarship and eyewitness accounts that would not have been available when he wrote the book. In addition to the titles mentioned above, I have found "The Diary of James Clegg", and "Witness to Rebellion - John Maclean's Journal of the 'Forty-Five" particularly valuable. There is also one title that was available only three years after Simpson's book was published that he would have found most useful -"Storm and Peace" by John Beresford, a series of historical essays of which the longest and most useful is "The Crisis of 1745" which includes lengthy and hitherto unpublished extracts from the archives at Chatsworth which casts new light on the government's response and which I have referred to in Chapter 5.

In addition to the text, I have taken the opportunity of adding a number of appendices. Some of these were published in Eardley-Simpson's book, but as this has been long out of print and is not easy to obtain, I wanted to make them available again. Some are completely new and will, I hope, cast fresh light on the events in Derby in December 1745, notably the lengthy "Relation of William Bateman". A further appendix gives details of the strength, composition and origin of all the Jacobite regiments that marched to Derby, and I have appended short biographies of the main characters involved by way of a "Dramatis Personae". Finally, I have added a chronology of events which I hope will help to put everything into context and will act as a convenient guide to the reader in unravelling these complex series of events.

My conclusions in the final chapter as to the Prince's prospects of success if he had continued his march to London, differ radically from Eardley-Simpson and, indeed, from other more recent writers, including the distinguished historian of the military aspects of the rebellion, Dr Christopher Duffy, and I offer them with some diffidence. I suspect that Eardley-Simpson would be strongly opposed to my views and would most certainly have embarked on a spirited debate as he did in the pages of the Derbyshire Archaeological and Natural History Society Journal in 1934 (see note 86 on p.102); I can only hope that by adopting a contrary view I have not aroused his shade to anger! Whatever view you take of the '45, it was a remarkable occurrence and I hope that the reader will enjoy the drama and excitement of the story and that it will cause them to look at the surviving 18th century buildings of Derby in a new light as they perambulate down Irongate following in the footsteps of the "Bonnie Prince".

As always, I owe an enormous debt of gratitude to the many people who have assisted in the writing of this book. In particular I wish to thank the staff at the Local Studies Library in Derby who have helped with a number of bibliographic enquiries, and the staff of the Derbyshire County Record Office who have supplied me with a number of interesting contemporary documents, one of which is reproduced at Appendix 8. My good friend Val Spotswood, whose eagle eye for the infelicitous phrase and the misplaced apostrophe has saved me from many errors of grammar, syntax and punctuation. Two people deserve special mention; Dr Eveline Cruickshanks, the doyenne of modern Jacobite studies, who has most generously allowed me to use her unpublished research materials on the role of the spy Dudley Bradstreet at the Council of War in Derby which have enabled me to lay to rest the long-standing myth that his attendance at the Council persuaded the Jacobites to retreat from Derby. Dr Jonathan Oates, member of the Jacobite Studies Trust and prolific author on Jacobite affairs, has kindly read the first draft of the manuscript in its entirety, thus saving me from many egregious errors of fact and interpretation, and has been a tower of strength throughout in providing me with many essential sources and helpful comments. This book could not have been written without him and he has my profound gratitude and thanks. A number of publishers have kindly allowed me to quote from their works that are still in copyright; in that connection I express my thanks to Tuckwell Press Ltd (now part of Birlinn Ltd) for permission to quote from "Witness to

Rebellion - John Maclean's Journal of the 'Forty-Five", to The Derbyshire Record Society for permission to quote from "The Diaries of James Clegg of Chapel en le Frith 1708-1755" and to Cassell Ltd for their permission to reproduce five of the maps from "The '45" by Christopher Duffy. Last, but not by any means least, I wish to thank my good friend Dave Mitchell of Scarthin Books who was enthusiastic about this project from the word go and has helped to steer it to its final publication. It goes without saying that any errors that remain are entirely my own responsibility.

A note on spelling, names, dates and money

This book contains a large number of eyewitness and contemporary accounts of the rebellion. In all of these I have left the spelling, grammar and punctuation unaltered from the sources from which they were transcribed. In many cases this is the original 18th century source which uses the style current at the time. It is hoped that readers will not find this off-putting, but once you get used to the fact that 18th century writers used capital initial letters lavishly (usually for a noun), then it is fairly easy to follow; rightly or wrongly I felt that to tamper with the spelling would detract from the authenticity of the piece.

There are a considerable number of Scottish names in this book, and no single source agrees on the correct spelling for many of them e.g. should it be McDonald, MacDonald, Macdonald, MacDonnell - the whole thing is a minefield in which the writer lays himself open to harsh criticism whatever option he chooses! I have therefore taken the coward's way out and used the spelling most commonly adopted in each case by previous writers. There are one or two English names which give rise to similar problems, notably Francis Townley whose name is spelt both Townley and Towneley. I have adopted the former spelling because it accords with the spelling used by most historians of the rising.

Dates are always a problem prior to the mid-eighteenth century. At the time of these events Great Britain still used the Julian Calendar, unlike many European powers which had already adopted the Gregorian Calendar (which we still use today). From 1700 there was a difference of 11 days between the two i.e. the Gregorian Calendar was adopted by Britain on 2nd September 1752 so the following day became 14th September. In this book all of the dates are those applicable under the Julian Calendar, commonly referred to as Old Style (OS), so they will reflect the dates actually applicable at the time.

Money raises its ugly head from time to time. I have made no attempt (because it is virtually impossible) to equate the sums referred to with modern values, but for the curious, and as a very rough approximation, if you multiply by about 200 it will give you some idea of the value today. For those unfamiliar with the pre-decimal system (and I am painfully aware that only those of us over 60 have any real recollection of it!), I have inserted the decimal value in parentheses.

Chapter 1

The Jacobite background

The origins of the Jacobite movement that brought Bonnie Prince Charlie's army to Derby in December 1745 lie a century earlier in the civil wars which ended in 1651. In January of 1649 King Charles I was tried by Parliament for treason, condemned to death and beheaded on a scaffold erected outside the Banqueting House in Whitehall. He was the second Stuart monarch of England, the son of James I who came to the throne of England in 1603 on the death of Queen Elizabeth I. James's mother was Mary Queen of Scots, executed at Fotheringhay in 1587, after a long imprisonment in England, on the order of her cousin, the same Queen Elizabeth whose throne James now occupied. Mary had been a devout Catholic; James, however, brought up in Scotland in his mother's absence by a coterie of Presbyterian Scottish lords, was bitterly anti-Catholic. During his reign, particularly after the abortive Gunpowder Plot in 1605, the penal laws against Catholics, first introduced by Elizabeth, continued to be enforced with rigour.

James's death brought his son Charles to the throne in 1625. Charles had none of his father's strict Presbyterianism; on the contrary, he inclined towards a High Anglican strain of the Church of England, what people would now refer to as Anglo-Catholicism. He appointed as Archbishop of Canterbury William Laud who was responsible for introducing reforms which turned the Church of England towards far more "Catholic" practice and ritual – for example by placing communion tables permanently at the east end of the chancel fenced off from the congregation by rails, insistence on the wearing of the surplice by the priest at communion services, a rigid adherence to the Thirty Nine Articles and, later, the introduction of a new prayer book to Scotland. All of this made his low-church Protestant subjects extremely uneasy and exacerbated his relations with them, and, to compound his difficulties, he was married to a French Catholic queen, Henrietta Maria. This led, almost inevitably, to the suspicion that the King intended, at some stage, to reintroduce Catholicism to England, and ultimately those tensions led to the Civil War that broke out in August of 1642.

After the defeat of the King's armies in the first (1642-1646) and second (1648) civil wars and his execution, his elder son Charles again took up arms against the victorious parliamentary forces from his base in Scotland where he had made a Faustian pact with the Scottish

Parliament to introduce Presbyterianism to England as the price of their support. In 1651 he invaded England with a Scots army getting as far as Worcester. Here he met the battle-hardened veterans of Cromwell's New Model Army, and on 3rd September they inflicted a decisive defeat on him. Charles fled to the continent (via the famous oak tree), and there he and his followers languished in exile for the next ten years, first in France and later at the Hague in Holland.

In 1660, however, in a surprising and unexpected change of fortune, Charles was restored to the throne. His restoration had been orchestrated by erstwhile supporters of Cromwell's Republic, disillusioned by the chaos and incompetence which followed Cromwell's death in 1658. Sensing that the mood of the people favoured a return to the old regime, General George Monck, later Duke of Albemarle, marched on London with his army, overthrew the Rump Parliament and called for free elections. Almost inevitably this led to an invitation to the King to return to his birthright. Amidst much popular acclamation Charles II landed at Dover on 25th May 1660 and would reign for the next twenty-five years.

His position was a difficult one. His country was still riven by the divisions of the Civil War and there was much suspicion that he intended to re-introduce Catholicism. This persistent strain in British politics, coupled with the inability of the Stuarts to produce legitimate heirs, was ultimately to lead to the end of their dynasty and to yet another civil war, this time not in England but in Scotland and Ireland.

However, in spite of his difficulties Charles managed to retain his throne by a mixture of tact, charm and devious political manoeuvring. In 1669 he entered into the secret Treaty of Dover with the French King Louis XIV. Under this treaty he agreed, amongst other things, to relieve Catholics of the penal laws under which they had suffered for so long, to reintroduce Catholicism as the national religion, and to announce his own conversion to Catholicism in his own time; in return he was promised money (three million livres per year – about £250,000) and up to 6,000 troops to suppress any internal disorder that might arise on the part of his disgruntled Protestant subjects. If the treaty had become general knowledge, there is little doubt that the overwhelmingly Protestant people of Britain would have been outraged and the King might well have lost his throne, but in fact Charles was content to take the money without fulfilling the other terms.

Charles died in 1685, converted to Catholicism on his deathbed by Father Huddleston. He left no legitimate heirs, so on his death he was succeeded by his younger brother James. James II had none of Charles' personal charm or charisma. Furthermore, he was an open Catholic who made no secret of his desire to reintroduce Catholicism and to repeal the anti-Catholic penal laws. These included two "Test Acts". The first Test Act of 1673 had debarred Catholics from any civil or military office under the crown; they could not, for example, obtain a commission in the army or navy, sit as magistrates or judges, or, indeed, practise as lawyers. They were also disenfranchised from voting for members of parliament. The second Test Act of 1678 excluded Catholic MP's from the House of Commons. James was determined to repeal these statutes, or at least to circumvent them, and to re-establish his Catholic subjects on equal terms with their Protestant neighbours. He began to issue commissions in the army to Catholics in defiance of the Test Acts, a decision upheld by the courts in the case of Godden -v- Hales, to surround himself with Catholic advisers and he also sought to repeal the Test Acts.

By July of 1688 tensions between the crown and the people had reached boiling point. The conflict was exacerbated by a Declaration of Indulgence issued by James on 7th May granting complete freedom of worship to Catholics, and ordered to be read in all the churches of the land. The hierarchy of the Church of England refused, and seven of the bishops, including the Archbishop of Canterbury, William Sancroft, presented a petition to the king and were imprisoned in the Tower for their temerity. The last straw was the birth of an heir, later James III (VIII of Scotland), on 10th June. This would mean that the Catholic Stuart dynasty would be perpetuated, and the more cynical opponents of the Crown put it about that the child was a changeling who had been smuggled into the queen's bedchamber in a warming-pan. Two months later some of the most notable Whig peers of the realm met at the Cock and Pynot Inn at Old Whittington near Chesterfield in Derbyshire (now called "Revolution House") to plot the overthrow of James II and his replacement by a Protestant monarch. They decided to offer the throne to Prince William of Orange, the Stadtholder of Holland who was married to James's eldest daughter, Mary. One of the most prominent conspirators was William Cavendish, 4th Earl of Devonshire, whose family seat was at Chatsworth in Derbyshire; for his part in the plot he was later elevated to Duke by a grateful King William. A deputation was sent to William to offer him the throne; he accepted and on 5th November 1688 he arrived at Torbay with fifty ships and an army of 13,000 men. James, his nerve broken and believing that his position was hopeless, fled abroad and the "Glorious Revolution" had been peacefully achieved. Peacefully, at least, in England (apart from one small skirmish)

– in other parts of the country the revolution took a more violent form. From his exile in France James recruited many Irish Catholics into his army, together with many Scots highland Catholics and Episcopalians. In Ireland a savage war ensued between the forces of James and William, known as the Jacobite War (the Latin for James is Jacobus and appears in that form on coinage of the realm, state papers and the Great Seal – hence James's supporters were known as Jacobites). In July 1690 James and his army were defeated at the Battle of the Boyne, and after further fighting the war was ended by the Treaty of Limerick in 1691. By this treaty Catholic Irish supporters of James were free to seek their fortunes abroad, and some 12,000 left to serve in the armies of France, Spain, Russia and even Sweden; this exodus became known as the "Flight of the Wild Geese" and it initiated a long tradition of Irish men and officers serving in foreign armies, particularly those of France and Spain. Indeed, in France so many of them joined up that an "Irish Brigade" was established – members of this brigade were later to serve in Bonnie Prince Charlie's army. By 1695 Parliament had enacted further penal laws against the Catholics and the "Protestant ascendancy" was once more firmly established in Ireland.

In Scotland, meanwhile, the heartland of support for the exiled Stuart monarchy, many Catholic highland clans found a charismatic leader in John Graham of Claverhouse, Viscount Dundee, known to his supporters as "Bonnie Dundee" and to his enemies as "Bluidy Clavers". On 27th July 1689 a Jacobite highland army led by Dundee swept down on a government army commanded by General Hugh MacKay in the Pass of Killiecrankie and cut it to pieces, but at the height of the battle Bonnie Dundee was shot and killed. Without his inspired leadership, the morale of the Jacobite army suffered a catastrophic decline and they were defeated at Dunkeld on 21st August after a bloody encounter with government troops. The Jacobite War in Scotland was effectively at an end.

The end of the Jacobite Wars in Scotland and Ireland, however, did not mean the end of Jacobite ambitions to restore James to the throne. In the years after the battles of the Boyne and Killiecrankie, there were many attempts to raise rebellion against William III and his successors, some more successful than others. From his court in exile at Versailles, James never ceased to plot and scheme his return to what he regarded as his God-given kingdom of Britain. James, like his father before him, was a firm believer in the "divine right of monarchy"; a king, once crowned and anointed, was the elected of God and could not validly be deposed. This notion, already outdated in England by the turn of the 18th Century, would condemn him and his successors to several lifetimes of forlorn and doomed attempts to restore their family to power in a country that had moved on into a more modern concept of kingship, and where the majority of the people, whilst some of them might remain uncomfortable with the way that James had been deposed and exiled, were not prepared to hazard their lives and fortunes to restore him.

On 16th September 1701, James died, to be succeeded, as far as Jacobites were concerned, by his son, also James, known to his supporters as James III/VIII and to his opponents as "the Old Pretender". His succession coincided with the start of a major war between France and her allies Spain and Bavaria on the one hand, and Britain and her allies Austria, Prussia and Holland on the other; this was the War of the Spanish Succession. Henceforward the hopes and aspirations of the Jacobites became firmly bound up with the need for French support. Jacobite fortunes rose or fell with the state of relations between France and Britain – when the two countries were at war then Jacobites could realistically look for French support, financial and military; when peace came, their hopes dwindled. Without French support the prospect of a Stuart restoration faded into nothing more than sentimental nostalgia and wishful thinking.

The war between France and England, therefore, began to re-kindle hopes of a successful rising in favour of King James. William III had died in March 1702 having contracted pneumonia brought on by injuries sustained in a riding accident when his horse stumbled over a mole hill, hence the toast of Jacobite supporters to "the little gentleman in the black velvet waistcoat". His sister in law, Anne, another of James II's sisters, succeeded him. Troubled by the strength of Stuart support in Scotland, her ministers determined to unify the two kingdoms under one parliament; this would involve abolishing the independently-minded Scottish parliament which they regarded as a potential focus for sedition and rebellion. In early 1707, by a judicious mixture of cajolery, intimidation and bribery, the Scottish Parliament was persuaded to vote itself out of existence. Under the Act of Union Scotland would now be represented by 45 MP's and 16 Lords sitting in the Parliament at London. Ireland continued to have its own independent parliament until 1801.

Although the Union was welcomed by many Scots, particularly Whig gentry and merchants, it was resented by others, and riots and unrest followed. It led directly to the abortive rebellion of 1708, "the First Jacobite Rebellion", in which an invasion fleet of French ships, with James and 6,000 French troops on board, sailed for Scotland intending to land on the Firth of Forth. The invasion was thwarted by a squadron of Royal Navy ships commanded by Admiral Byng (father of the infamous Admiral Byng executed by firing squad in 1757 for losing the Island of Majorca to the French). The rising never got off the ground and James and the invasion force returned to France with nothing achieved.

The next attempt at a rising by the Jacobites, however, was a much more serious affair. This was the Jacobite Rebellion of 1715, commonly referred to as "the '15", and some of its participants would be out again in 1745 in support of Bonnie Prince Charlie. In 1713 the long War of the Spanish Succession with France was ended by the Treaty of Utrecht. One of its provisions stipulated that the exiled court of the Stuarts be expelled from France, and in September of that year they were banished to Lorraine. The Duke of Orleans, who effectively ruled France as Regent during the minority of Louis XV (Louis XIV having died some months earlier), was determined that the peace between Britain and France should endure so that France could recover from the terrible social and economic damage inflicted on it by the incessant warfare of the past twelve years. He was distinctly lukewarm in his support of the Old Pretender, but encouragement for his cause emerged from a different quarter. On 1st August 1714 Queen Anne died. She had enjoyed a long and relatively happy marriage with Prince George of Denmark but had suffered numerous miscarriages. Those children who survived had died in infancy or childhood, the last one aged 13 in 1700, so on her death she left no living heir. This created problems in the succession which the government had sought to anticipate by passing the Act of Settlement in 1701. This provided that no Roman Catholic could succeed to the throne, so on Anne's death the succession went to her nearest Protestant relative. He happened to be George, Elector of Hanover, who was the great-great-grandson of Mary Queen of Scots by his mother Sophia. His accession marked the start of what became known as the Hanoverian dynasty.

George was completely German in culture, background and upbringing. He spoke no English and, although supported by many of his subjects because he was a Protestant, was equally disliked by many as a German-speaking foreigner who didn't understand them. His accession gave much additional impetus to the Jacobite cause. In Scotland John Erskine, Earl of Mar, raised the Jacobite standard at Braemar on 6th September 1715 and the second, and most dangerous, Jacobite Rebellion was under way.

What made this rising such a serious threat was not just its widespread support in Scotland, both among the population at large and among the aristocrats and leading gentry, but the extent of support in England; unlike the rising of 1745, the insurgents could confidently expect significant numbers of recruits if they were to attempt an invasion of England.

Initially the government troops were outnumbered and taken by surprise, and Mar quickly took control of most of Scotland. One of his earliest and most enthusiastic adherents was the 21 year old Lord George Murray who would later play such an important role in Bonnie Prince Charlie's army and in the decision of the Council of War at Derby. He raised and commanded a regiment of clansmen from his family estates in Atholl as, indeed, he would do again in 1745. In the meantime a small Jacobite force of about 2,000 men, under Viscount Kenmure and Thomas Forster MP, in a strange presentiment of what would happen thirty years later, invaded England, reaching as far as Preston. Here they fought a fierce, but inconclusive, battle for two days against superior numbers of government troops under General Carpenter, and eventually surrendered on 14th November. The English Jacobites, on their march south, had confidently expected to be joined by large numbers of supporters. In the event these never materialised and they were able to raise very few new recruits save for a small number of mainly Catholic gentry and their retainers who joined them at Lancaster and Preston–again a curious echo of Bonnie Prince Charlie's experience in 1745. The surrender of the Jacobites at Preston had been preceded a day earlier by a drawn battle in Scotland at Sheriffmuir on 13th November when the main Jacobite army under Mar met the government troops commanded by the leader of the Scottish Whigs, John Campbell, 2nd Duke of Argyll, known as "Red John of the Battles". Although, in truth, neither side could claim a victory, and the rebellion spluttered on for a further three months, the battle effectively spelt the end of the rising. In spite of the successful landing of James in Scotland on 22nd December, the rebels, faced with strong government forces and much reduced in numbers and morale, broke up and dispersed in February 1716 and the leaders fled abroad or were captured and executed. The Earl of Nithsdale made a dramatic escape from prison with the assistance of his wife and disguised in her clothes, and his colleague the Earl of Derwentwater was executed. The second Jacobite Rebellion, and the most serious challenge so far to the Hanoverian dynasty, was at an end, and Jacobite hopes were dashed once more. [1]

Four years later there was yet another attempt at an armed restoration of the Stuarts, the Third Jacobite Rebellion of 1719. This time James had allied himself with the Spanish. Britain was at war with Spain, and in December 1718 Admiral Byng had defeated the Spanish Mediterranean fleet at Cape Passaro with heavy loss. In revenge, the Spanish supported a landing of Spanish troops in England and a further invasion of Scotland under the Earl Marischal, George Keith. At the same time William Murray, Marquis of Tullibardine (brother of Lord George Murray), formerly the Duke of Atholl whose title had been forfeit to the crown, set sail from France and the two met on the Isle of Lewis on 14th April 1719. By 13th April the combined force of Spanish together with some 1,600 MacDonalds and Camerons were at Loch Alsh. Forty of the Spanish troops garrisoned Eilean Donan Castle, but were bombarded by Royal Navy vessels on Loch Alsh and forced to surrender. The castle was blown up when a shell hit the magazine and the garrison was captured. Two months later the rebel army was defeated and dispersed at the Battle of Glenshiel on 10th June, and once more an armed rebellion by supporters of King James had been defeated. There was not to be another rising until the meteoric rise of Bonnie Prince Charlie some thirty years later.

For the next twenty-six years, Jacobite supporters lay low, launching occasional ineffective plots and hoping against hope for French support, nursing their grievances and planning their schemes in Jacobite drinking clubs where they could safely drink their disloyal toasts to "the King over the water". It seemed as if any serious military threat to the Hanoverian dynasty was over for good.

Chapter 2

The Progress of the Rising up to November 1745

When Bonnie Prince Charlie first set foot on Eriskay on 23rd July 1745, his natural optimism and buoyancy must surely have been tested, both by the events of the previous few months and by the stormy and inauspicious weather which accompanied him. Charles himself was only 25 years old, gauche in many ways, but enthusiastic and imbued with confidence in his ability to wrest his father's crown from the Hanoverian usurpers.

He had been born on 20th December 1720, only a year after the last abortive Jacobite rebellion, and was christened, to give him his full battery of names, Charles Edward Louis John Casimir Sylvester Severino Maria Stuart. His birth was cause for celebration at the court of his father James Francis Stuart "the Old Pretender" and his mother Clementina Sobieska, a Polish princess – here at last was a male heir for the Stuarts in whom all their hopes of a restoration could be vested. [2]

By this time the Stuart court, shunned by most of the states of Europe, was living in Rome under the protection of Pope Benedict XIV. Charles was brought up in what has been described as "a loving but disputatious family", but unfortunately, while he was still quite young, his mother began to display signs of mental instability, exacerbated by the birth of his brother Henry in 1725. This was later to confine her to an asylum for much of her life. As a consequence his parents became estranged and Clementina died in 1735. By the time he reached his early teens, the Prince was a tall, well-built and handsome young man who had had his martial ambitions fired by his attendance, at the age of 13, at the Siege of Gaeta. Thereafter he embarked on a rigorous course of physical exercise in preparation for a military life, riding and walking long distances, and by the time he landed in Eriskay he was of a sturdy, tireless and energetic disposition with much of the Stuart charm of his great-uncle, Charles II which had somehow bypassed both his father and grandfather.

However optimistic Charles might have been about the prospects of a Stuart restoration, by the second quarter of the 18th Century there was no longer a realistic possibility of it succeeding without substantial foreign help – and that meant assistance from France, Britain's traditional enemy. The problem for Charles was that the Treaty of Utrecht had established what appeared to be a lasting peace between the two countries, and from 1715 onwards that peace remained unbroken for more than twenty-five years, the longest peace between France and Britain since 1688. In 1739, however, Britain went to war with Spain, the so-called "War of Jenkin's Ear" and in 1743 the conflict widened to include France as well in the War of the Austrian Succession. Now at last the exiled Jacobite court could take heart from the hope of French military intervention in support of their cause.

In the autumn of 1743 the French king, Louis XV, planned a large-scale invasion of Britain. It was to be a two-pronged attack: one fleet with 3,000 men under the Earl Marischal, who had been a prime mover in the '15, was to land in Scotland and raise the highland clans in support of James, while the larger force of 12,000 under the command of France's premier soldier, Marshal Maurice de Saxe, was to sail from Dunkirk and land on the south coast of England. All these brave hopes came to naught when the fickle English Channel weather intervened in favour of the Royal Navy. On 24th February 1744 a strong fleet of ships appeared off Dunkirk to harass and delay the embarkation of the troops; that same night a strong wind blew up wrecking and dispersing most of the French fleet. It was a replay of what had happened more than 150 years earlier to the Spanish Armada, and as a result the plans for the expedition were abandoned. In January 1744 Charles went secretly to Gravelines to join the invasion, but by the autumn of that year it was clear that hopes of a French landing in England had been dashed and were unlikely to be revived in the foreseeable future. The French wanted a victory over Britain, but they wanted it cheaply and it was clear that, at best, the French government was ambivalent about landing on the enemy's coast in the face of a powerful Royal Navy with all the attendant risks and uncertainties that that involved.

Charles therefore boldly decided to make the attempt himself without French support. He travelled to Paris and, on the strength of a large advance from his father's bankers (it is unclear whether James knew or approved of this), he engaged the services of two Franco-Irish privateers at St Malo. These were the descendants of those Irish Jacobites, the "wild geese" who had fled Ireland for France under the terms of the Treaty of Limerick after their defeat in the Jacobite War. They had a long history of service to the French crown in both the navy, mainly as privateers, and in the Irish Brigade. At this time the Brigade numbered some 6,000 men in the Regiments of Dillon, Lally, Berwick, Bulkeley, Rooth, Clare and the Royal Ecossais and was the flower of the French army. They had fought against their own countrymen in the War of the Spanish Succession and were now doing so again in the War of the

Austrian Succession, and with a long-standing enmity towards the Williamite and Hanoverian dynasties, were only too ready to continue their war on the British crown.

The Anglo-Irish to whom Charles turned for help were happy to assist him, at a price. Sir Walter Routledge provided a captured 64 gun British ship *The Elisabeth* and his colleague Antoine Walsh lent the *Du Teillay* on which the Prince sailed from Belle Isle on 22nd June 1745. *The Elisabeth* joined them from Brest and they sailed in company to their intended landfall on the west coast of Scotland. The *Elisabeth* carried the bulk of the arms which the Prince had purchased with his father's money – 1,500 muskets and 1,800 broadswords – and, in addition, 700 French regular volunteers from Clare's Regiment of the Irish Brigade, no doubt seen by the French government as a cheap and expendable investment in a military adventure that must have seemed at the time to be something of a forlorn hope. The Prince himself sailed on the *Du Teillay* with the rest of the muskets, 4,000 Louis D'Ors in gold, and the ship's adventurous owner, Antoine Walsh.

All seemed to be going well and the expedition was just celebrating its escape from the patrolling British ships when, on 9th July, off the Scillies, they were unlucky enough to encounter the Royal Navy Man of War *HMS Lyon*. A savage battle ensued between *Lyon* and *Elisabeth* in which, as her captain Brett noted in his log "[the *Lyon*] received a great many shot in her hull which killed 45 men...and 107 were disabled with wounds". Antoine Walsh observed the battle at close quarters from the quarterdeck of the *Du Teillay*:-

"The Englishman, being to windward of the *Elisabeth*, hauled down his mizzen and hoisted his jib. The *Elisabeth*, having delayed a little in executing the same manoeuvre, the Englishman had time to pass forward, and contrived so well that he fired all his port volley, which raked the *Elisabeth* fore and aft, and must have killed many and done her great damage, so that the Englishman got between our two ships, and fired from his starboard guns three shots, which passed between my masts; my sails were riddled with his small shot, so much so that we did not fire, being out of range to meet him with our small guns." [3]

The *Elisabeth* was so badly damaged that she had no option but to return to port in France with all of the arms and the Irish volunteers, leaving Charles in the *Du Teillay* to sail on alone, surely thinking now that his efforts must be doomed before they had really begun. Nevertheless they sailed on, and the Prince made landfall at

Eriskay, in a strong gale with heavy rain, on 23rd July 1745. He had with him only the few arms carried by the *Du Teillay*, the money he had raised, and seven close companions, known to history as "the seven men of Moidart" - his elderly Irish tutor Sir Thomas Sheridan, then aged 70 and in poor health, William, titular Duke of Atholl, deposed owing to his support for the Jacobites in the '15, Aeneas MacDonald, a banker with strong family connections to the MacDonalds of the Western Isles, Francis Strickland, an English Jacobite from Cumberland, also in poor health (he died during the course of the campaign), George Kelly, an Irish clergyman, John William O'Sullivan, once a candidate for the priesthood, but now a career soldier in the Irish Brigade, and the elderly and irascible alcoholic Sir John MacDonald, sometime officer in the Scots Regiment of the French Army, the Royal Ecossais. With these slender, and in terms of personnel, rather alarming, resources, the Prince still hoped to raise a rebellion in Scotland that would topple the British government and the Hanoverian dynasty and restore his father to the throne.

Initially his reception was a cool one. He spent his first night at a croft belonging to Angus MacDonald. Aeneas MacDonald recounted the story in his journal:-

"The Prince, not being accustomed to...fires in the middle of the room, and there being no other chimney than a hole in the roof, was almost choaked, and was obliged to go often to the door for fresh air. This at last made the landlord, Angus MacDonald, call out, "What a plague is the matter with that fellow, that he can neither sit nor stand still, and neither keep within nor without doors?" [4]

On the following day Alexander MacDonald of Boisdale, brother of the chief of Clanranald, rowed over from South Uist to meet the Prince, and gave him discouraging news about the prospect of support in the islands. The Prince had hoped that he might be able to rely on both Sir Alexander MacDonald of Sleat and Norman MacLeod of Dunvegan (two prominent local clan chiefs) to bring out their clansmen for the cause. However, both were supporters of the Hanoverian regime and, in any event, were being blackmailed by the Lord President of the Council; this was the senior government representative in Scotland, Duncan Forbes of Culloden, who had become aware that they were shipping off their clansmen to North America as indentured servants. He had threatened them with criminal proceedings if they supported the Prince, and they remained aloof from the rising.

There is a lively pen portrait of the Prince at this time which admirably conveys the character of the young man whose charm and self-possession was soon to bring out highland clansmen in droves in his support:-

"A tall youth of a most agreeable aspect in a plain black coat, with a plain shirt, not very clean, and a cambric stock fixed with a plain silver buckle, a plain hatt with a canvas string having one end fixed to one of his coat buttons; he had black stockings and brass buckles in his shoes; at his first appearance, I found my heart swell to my very throat." [5]

Moving to the mainland at Loch nan Uamh on 25th July, the Prince quickly won over to his side the MacDonalds of Clanranald, the MacDonalds of Glencoe ("a turbulent clan"), and the MacDonalds of Keppoch. However, his hopes of attracting the support of the powerful Clan Cameron under their chief Donald Cameron of Lochiel, "the Gentle Lochiel" as he was universally known, remained unfulfilled when the chief prevaricated and, after meeting the Prince, left him without making any definite pledge of support.

Gathering his few clansmen about him, therefore, the Prince marched for Glenfinnan at the head of Loch Shiel, where the 1719 rebellion had been extinguished twenty-six years before. Here he and his supporters waited for the Camerons to appear and join them. After an agonised wait of several hours, at last they heard the skirl of bagpipes, and the Camerons came into view, Lochiel at their head. It was a decisive shift in the momentum of the rebellion – from a few dedicated and romantic Jacobite supporters into the beginnings of what would become a formidable fighting force that would pose a serious threat to George II. An eyewitness gives a vivid account of the occasion:-

"The Camerons advanced in two lines (each of them three men deep). Between the lines were the soldiers taken on the 16th, marching as prisoners without their arms. Charles, elevated with the sight of such a clan (for the Camerons are said to have been 700 or 800 men that day, many of them without arms) proceeded immediately to erect the standard. The Marquis of Tullibardine [the Duke of Atholl to Jacobites] unfurled the standard; and, supported by a man on each side, held the staff till the manifest and commission of regency were read, both dated at Rome, December 1743. In an hour or two after this solemnity, MacDonnell of Keppoch arrived with about 300 men. In the evening of the same day, some gentlemen of the name of MacLeod came to

Glenfinnan, who disclaimed their chief, and offered themselves to return to the Isles, and raise all the men they could for the service of their Prince." [6]

From Glenfinnan, Charles and his little army, now some 1,800 strong, marched to Aberchalder. Here, on 27th August, he carried out a review of his troops and was joined by the Grants of Glenmoriston and the MacDonnells of Glengarry. The next day the Jacobites occupied the strategically important Corryairack Pass, making an abortive attempt to capture the government barracks at Ruthven, garrisoned by Sgt Molloy of Lee's 55th Regiment and twelve men, who successfully held them off.

By now the government had become aware, and was becoming increasingly alarmed, about events in the highlands. As early as 1st August they put a price of £30,000 on the Prince's head and on 17th August the London Gazette reported:-

> "A ship of 18 guns had appeared on the west coast of
> Scotland; which, after having cruised for some days off the
> island of Bara [sic] and Uist, stood in for the coast of Lochaber;
> and had there landed, betwixt the island of Mull and Skie [sic],
> several persons; one of whom, from the general report, and
> from several concurring circumstances, there is the greatest
> reason to believe is the Pretender's son."

The commander of the government troops in Scotland was Lieutenant General Sir John Cope. His forces were slender – five companies of Lee's 55th Regiment, most of Lascelles' 58th Regiment, Murray's 57th Regiment and two companies of the highland 42nd Regiment, the Black Watch, perhaps 2,000 in total. As the Prince's army was marching from Glenfinnan, Cope marched his infantry up to Stirling, leaving behind his two regiments of dragoons, Gardiner's and Hamilton's, which were encamped in and around Edinburgh. From Stirling he marched north to Crieff and Dalnacardoch, along the roads built by his predecessor, Major General Wade, in order to meet the rebels as they debouched from the highlands. However, on the way he received an alarming (and, as it happened, false) report of the strength of the Jacobite forces that had established themselves on the heights of the Corryairack Pass. At a council of war he and his officers agreed that it would be too dangerous to try and force the pass with the troops at their disposal, and they took the fateful decision to by-pass it and to march instead to Inverness where they could support the pro-government Whig clans of the north east highlands. Cope reached Inverness on 29th August, leaving open the road to Edinburgh and the central lowlands to Charles's highland army. Seizing the opportunity, Charles marched his army to Perth, and on 4th September welcomed some important new recruits, including the man who was to be one of his most experienced commanders, and the architect of the invasion of England, Lord George Murray, the younger brother of the Jacobite Duke of Atholl and of his brother James, 2nd Duke of Atholl who was recognised by the government. This was to be, in many ways, another civil war, dividing both families and friends. Here the Prince was also joined by many of the senior Jacobite commanders that would march with him to Derby: James Drummond, Duke of Perth, David Ogilvie, titular Earl of Airlie, and a long-standing Jacobite supporter, Oliphant of Gask, William Drummond Lord Strathallan, and Struan, chief of Clan Robertson, with 200 of his clansmen. Here also appears for the first time one of the liveliest and most interesting (but perhaps unreliable) chroniclers of the rising, James Chevalier de Johnstone, the twenty-six year old son of an Edinburgh merchant from a Jacobite family. He was immediately appointed as aide de camp to Lord George Murray. By 11th September the Jacobite army had crossed the Forth at the Fords of Frew and was poised to capture Edinburgh.

In 1745 the defences of Scotland's capital were weak; it had not had to face an enemy since 1689, and the city's lack of preparedness reflected this. There was a long wall around three sides of the city, the Flodden Wall, not easily defensible and certainly not proof against artillery fire or a determined assault. The garrison of the city consisted of a large but poorly trained regiment of militia, or volunteers, numbering some 900 men, who were in no state to meet the hardened warriors of the highland army on equal terms. The castle, situated on a plug of volcanic rock rising some 700 feet above the city, was virtually impregnable, but even its garrison gave cause for concern, consisting as it did of two companies only of Lascelles' 58th Regiment and a regiment of invalids (soldiers too old or infirm for active service) commanded by the 82 year old General Joshua Guest. The morale of the garrison and city militia was not improved when the two regiments of dragoons, left behind by Cope, took fright at the approach of the Jacobites and beat a hasty and undignified retreat, not stopping until they reached the little village of Prestonpans eight miles to the east of the city. The deputies of the city, under a flag of truce, came in a coach to seek terms from Charles but their proposals were rejected. In the early hours of 17th September, a picked band of Camerons under Lochiel approached the city walls near the gate known as the Nether Bow and managed to gain access by a ruse. The Prince's secretary, Murray of Broughton, wrote a lively account of what happened in his journal:-

"Lochiel ordered one of his people in a great coat and hunting cape to go and demand entrance att the gate, while he was ready to have followed him in case he had obtained admittance, but the fellow being refused access, and it now being clear daylight., Mr M[urray] proposed to retire to a place call'd St Leonard's hills, and after securing themselves from the cannon of the Castle, to waite for orders from the Chevalier [i.e. Prince Charles] where to attack the town... This retreat being thus agreed to, Mr M went to the rear of the detachment to make them march and guide them to the place proposed, but before he had time to get so far, the Coach which had returned with the Deputies came down the High Street, and oblidged the guard to open the Port, upon which Lochiel took the advantage and rushed in, the guard immediately dispersing. Thus did the Chevalier render himself master of the Capital without shedding a drop of blood." [7]

On the following day Charles entered the city and King James was proclaimed at the Mercat Cross. An anonymous loyalist, probably Patrick Crighton, an Edinburgh burgess, recorded the scene:-

"The Crosse to the east was covered with a larg fine Persian carpet. The Lyon Heralds in there formalities, coats on, and bleasons [blazons – a tabard with their insignia of office], came attended with but one trumpet to the theatur or to the Crosse...all the streat and the windows and forstairs weer crowded, and silence being made, the manefesto was read.....After all these, [the] military [were] dismissed with bagpipes playing and a fashion of streamers over ther showlders, and the chime of bells from the High Church steaple gave musicall tunes all the whill." [8]

There is an excellent description of the Prince at about this time by the Whig observer Andrew Henderson who later wrote a book about the rebellion:-

"He was a tall slender young Man, about five Feet ten Inches high, of a ruddy Complexion, high nosed, large rolling brown Eyes, long visaged, red-haired, but at that Time wore a pale Periwig. He was in

Highland Habit, had a blue Sash, wrought with Gold, that came over his Shoulder; red Velvet Breeches, a green Velvet Bonnet, with a white Cockade, and Gold Lace about it. He had a Silver-hilted broad Sword, and was shewn great Respect by his Forces." [9]

Meanwhile, at Inverness, Cope was marching his troops to Aberdeen and had sent for shipping to meet him there so that they could be transferred to the Firth of Forth to meet the growing threat to the capital from the highland army. On 15th September, just two days before the Jacobites entered Edinburgh, his fleet sailed from Aberdeen and on 16th landed at the little port of Dunbar. Three days later his forces were encamped at Haddington, to the east of the city, and the scene was set for the first major clash of the rebellion at Prestonpans.

Having established themselves in Edinburgh and proclaimed King James, on 20th September the Jacobite army marched to meet Cope, their men deploying on Falside Hill, a strong position overlooking Cope's army to the north. However, when the Jacobite commanders came to examine the field of battle more closely, it became clear that Cope's army was protected on its front by a deep ditch and hedge which would make the traditional highland charge extremely difficult; for this they needed an unimpeded run at the enemy, preferably across ground without significant obstacles such as bogs and tussocks. Such a "plain field" could be found directly to the east of the government army, so during the night the Jacobites marched east and then north and the early hours of 21st September found them deployed north to south and facing west with Cope's army directly in front of them but at right angles. On the march the Prince had stumbled and fallen into a ditch, regarded as a bad omen by his men, but the Prince made light of the incident and the march continued. Realising, almost too late, that the enemy was now threatening his left flank, Cope rapidly wheeled his army to face the Jacobites. The two armies were equally matched in numbers – the Jacobites probably totalled no more than about 2,400 men and the government troops about 2,200, but the highlanders were poorly armed at this stage, with few muskets, and only one artillery piece. Their opponents, by contrast, were well-armed with the "Brown Bess" musket, a cumbersome weapon to fire with an effective range of only 100 yards, but a most effective weapon when used in volleys, firing a one ounce ball and, in the hands of a trained man, capable of firing up to three rounds a minute. They also had a small park of artillery consisting of four mortars and six 1½lb guns. Their disadvantage was that many of the troops present on the field were raw recruits with very little training, and they had no trained artillerymen to man the guns. They now had to face the dreaded highland charge for the first time. This traditional highland tactic, indeed, in most cases their only tactic, was well described in The New Dictionary Geographical of 1760:-

"The highlandmen, when under their own management, still retain their ancient manner of fighting: for after they have fired a few shot, they throw off their plaids, which anciently little lads, who attended them, picked up, and with unabating ardour, and a rapidity like lightening, they run up, & come directly to close quarters, attacking their enemy with broadsword in hand."

As dawn broke, with a mist still hanging in the hollows, the Jacobite army appeared out of the murk charging at full speed towards the right of Cope's lines where the Dragoons of Hamilton and Gardiner were deployed. First into the fray were the Clan Donald Regiments of Keppoch, Clanranald and Glengarry. In an instant Cope's lines dissolved and his men were cut to pieces, save for one or two pockets of resistance which held out. Effectively the battle was all over in fifteen minutes. The Chevalier Johnstone gives a vivid account of this first overwhelming Jacobite victory:-

"Lord George [Murray] at the head of the first line, did not give the English time to recover from their surprise. He advanced with such rapidity that General Cope had hardly time to form his troops in order of battle, before the Highlanders rushed upon them sword in hand. They had been frequently enjoined to aim at the noses of the horses with their swords, without minding the riders, as the natural movement of a horse, wounded in the face, is to wheel round, and a few horses wounded in that manner are sufficient to throw a whole squadron into such disorder that it is impossible afterwards to rally it. They followed this advice most implicitly, and the English cavalry were instantly thrown into confusion. MacGregor's company did great execution with their scythes. They cut the legs of the horses in two, and their riders through the middle of their bodies. MacGregor was brave and intrepid, but, at the same time, altogether whimsical and singular. When advancing to the charge with his company, he received five wounds, two of them from balls that pierced his body through and through. Stretched on the ground, with his head resting on his hand, he called out to the Highlanders of his company, "My lads, I am not dead! By G--, I shall see if any of you does not do his duty!" The Highlanders instantly fell on the flanks of the infantry which, being uncovered and exposed from the flight of the cavalry, immediately gave way. Thus in less than five minutes, we obtained a complete victory, with terrible carnage on the part of the enemy." [10]

Battle casualties are always difficult to estimate accurately, but Cope's army probably suffered a total of about 1,400 killed and taken prisoner, including 80 officers; some 450 of his men escaped, and, in addition, the victorious Jacobites captured 2,000 muskets and all of Cope's artillery. This would accompany them two months later on their march to Derby. The Prince was jubilant at his first victory and his demeanour was noted by a Whig supporter, the schoolmaster Andrew Henderson:-

"I went to the road-side where the Chevalier....was standing. He was clad as an ordinary Captain, in a coarse plaid and blue bonnet, his boots and knees were much dirtied; he seemed to have fallen into a ditch, which I was told by one of his Lifeguards he had. He was exceeding merry: speaking of his army, he said twice, "My Highlandmen have lost their Plaids." At which he laughed very heartily. When talking of the wounded, he seemed in no way affected. There were seven standards taken, which when he saw, he said in French, a language he frequently spoke in, "We have missed some of them". Then he refreshed himself upon the field and with the utmost composure eat a piece of cold beef, and drank a glass of wine, amidst the deep and piercing groans of the wounded and dying, who had fallen a sacrifice to his ambition." [11]

After the battle the highland army remained in Edinburgh for six weeks to recover its strength. Here one of the regiments that accompanied Charles to Derby was recruited and trained. This was the Edinburgh Regiment, commanded by the long-standing Jacobite agent and adventurer John Roy Stewart who had served, like so many Jacobite officers, in the French regular army.

The highlanders had captured the city of Edinburgh but the castle still held out under the surprisingly robust leadership of the aged General Guest, and the Jacobite's quarters regularly came under fire from the castle's guns. The Prince installed himself and his retinue at the Royal Palace of Holyroodhouse, where his great great grandmother, Mary Queen of Scots, had witnessed the murder of her secretary David Rizzio in 1566. Here he entertained visitors, transacted business and held routs, dances and dinners for the great and the good of Jacobite society, of which there were many, Edinburgh being a notably Jacobite city, unlike Glasgow which was solidly Whig and for the government. On 30th September he was invested as a knight in the Scottish order of chivalry known as The Temple of Jerusalem; the Duke of Perth wrote to Lord Ogilvie:-

"It is truly a proud thing to see our Prince in the palace of his fathers, with all the best blood of Scotland around him. He is much beloved of all sorts, and we cannot fail to make that pestilent England smoke for it. Upon Monday last there was a great ball at the Palace, and on Tuesday, by appointment, there was solemn chapter of the ancient chivalry of the Temple of Jerusalem held in the audience room...Our noble Prince looked most gallantly in the white robe of the order, took his profession like a worthy knight, and, after receiving congratulations of all present, did avow that he would restore the Temple higher than it was in the days of William the Lion." [12]

He was also much in demand by the ladies of Edinburgh, "but", an observer said "his behaviour to them was very cool" and when he was asked to patronise balls he replied "Ladies, there a great many Balls abiding me, at present have me excused, but be sure of one after my return".

Clearly the Prince and his advisers now had an important decision to make: should they exploit their victory at Prestonpans by consolidating their hold on Scotland and recruiting and training a larger army to meet the inevitable response from the government, or should they maintain the impetus of victory by invading England with the resources currently available to them?

To oppose the Jacobites, the government had two armies, one based in Newcastle-upon-Tyne under the aged and decrepit Field Marshal Wade, and the other, still gathering, under General Ligonier in the Midlands. Supposing that they decided on invasion, which route should they take? Should they march down the east coast towards Newcastle and risk meeting Wade's army in battle, or should they march down the west coast through Cumberland and Westmorland where Jacobite agents had led them to believe that they would obtain much support from their English adherents?

These questions caused much discussion amongst the Jacobite High Command. One of the early historians of the rising, John Home, himself captured at the Battle of Falkirk the following year, described the Prince's style of command:-

"The Council mett regularly every morning in his drawing room....The Prince, in this Councill, used Always first to declare what he was for, and then he Ask'd Every body's opinion in their turn. Their was one third of the Councill whose principals were, that Kings and Princes Can never either act or think wrong; so, in Consequence, they always Confirmed whatever the Prince said. The other two thirds, who thought that Kings and Princes thought sometimes like other men, and were not altogether infallible, and that this Prince was no more so than others, beg'd leave to differ from him when they could give Sufficient reasons for their differences of Opinion. Which very often was no hard matter to do; for as the Prince and his Old Governor, Sir Thomas Sheridan, were altogether ignorant of the Ways and Customs in Great Britain, and both much for the Doctrine of Absolute monarchy, they would very often, had they not been prevented, have fall'n into Blunders which might have hurt the Cause. The Prince Could not bear to hear any body differ in Sentiment from him, and took a dislike to Every body that did; for he had a Notion of Commanding his army As any General does a body of Mercenaries, and so lett them know only what he pleased, and [expected them to] obey without inquiring further about the matter." [13]

This interesting analysis of the Prince's character is worth bearing in mind in relation to the critical Council of War at Derby. Charles was a young, impetuous, rather stiff-necked man, inexperienced in the way of the world but extremely conscious of his position. He did not react well to criticism or differences of opinion. This made military decisions amongst the Jacobite commanders exceedingly difficult and, as Home implies, led to cliques within the council which would later cause bitter dissension.

The Prince himself was much in favour of an immediate invasion of England; some of his senior commanders, however, were more cautious. In the end it was decided that an invasion of England would be mounted, but there was disagreement about the route to be taken. The final council meeting took place on 30th October 1745 and the Prince's secretary, John Murray of Broughton, recorded its proceedings in his journal:-

"The Prince called a Councill of war the night of [October] 30th, where were present his Grace the Duke of Athol, D of Perth, L George Murray, Lord Elcho, L Pitsligoe, Cameron of Lochiel, Mcdonald of Kepoch, Mcdonald of Clanronald, Mcdonald of Lochgaray etc, to consult of his march Southwards...wither to march the east road towards Newcastle, and there give General Wade Battle, or to march west by

Carlile. The Chevalier him self was clear for marching towards Newcastle......On the other hand my Lord George Murray, with most of the Cheifs, argued that his marching into England being Cheifly to give his friends there an opportunity to join him.....they was of opinion that by marching to Carlile and being there joined by his freinds from Lancashire, Northumberland etc as he expected, they might then Choose to march to NewCastle and give Mr Wade Battle or not as should be thought most advisable." [14]

The Prince deferred his decision until the following morning and then decided that the army would march by the western route to Carlisle. The highland army marched that very day towards England and their destiny at Derby.

Chapter 3

The Invasion of England

By the autumn of 1745, news of the Jacobite rising north of the border had filtered down even to the most remote parts of England. In Chapel-en-le-Frith, 65 year old James Clegg, who combined the roles of non-conformist minister and doctor, noted in his diary on 24th September "Today we hear the Scotch Rebels are in possession of the city of Edenburgh and for advancing towards England speedily". Two days later his entry reads "I had an account from my son James of the defeat of the King's forces by the Rebels in Scotland" and on the following day "All about in a great consternation under apprehensions of the progress of the Rebellion, our Gentlemen set out to meet the Duke of Devonshire at Derby to concert measures for raising forces for the defence of the nation"[15]. His entries become steadily more alarmed and anxious as the Jacobite army advanced into the northern counties of England.

As the rising began to gather momentum, the government hastily recalled troops from Flanders. After their shocking and unexpected defeat at Prestonpans, they at last began to realize the seriousness of the threat from Prince Charles's army and accelerated the return of the rest of their troops from the Low Countries where they had been heavily engaged in a campaign against the French. Only four months before they had fought and lost a ferocious battle at Fontenoy where they suffered 12,000 casualties including 3,000 men taken prisoner. By December the campaign had been abandoned and in a matter of weeks 4,200 Dutch and Swiss mercenary troops, three battalions of the Guards, 18 line regiments, 9 squadrons of cavalry and four companies of artillery had been hastily shipped back from the continent and were marching to deploy at Newcastle and in the Midlands.

The elderly and lethargic Wade however, was not the man to beat the hard-marching Jacobites who by now had both the advantage of the initiative and a strong element of surprise. By 9th November the Jacobite advance guard was already outside Carlisle and had sent the garrison a summons to surrender the town and castle. The summons received an immediate reply from the guns on the castle walls, and the following day the highlanders commenced siege operations. Initially the Jacobites were repulsed, but within days both the town and the castle had surrendered, Charles's army obtaining much needed muskets,

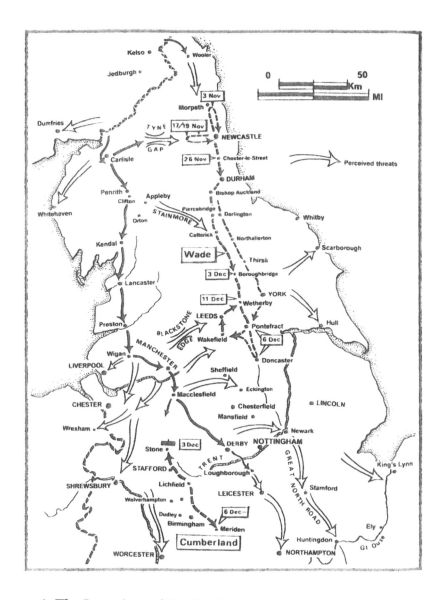

1. The Invasion of England ... with Feints and Panics

powder and ammunition. Such of the militia and invalids who had not already deserted were allowed to march free and on 15th November Charles entered Carlisle in triumph riding on a white charger and preceded by one hundred pipers.

On 18th November a council of war was held to decide on the Jacobites' next move. Its proceedings are summarised in his journal by the Prince's secretary, Murray of Broughton:-

"...a council of war was Called to determine of what was next to be done, and after some deliberation it was agreed on to march into Lancashire. Tho the Chevalier in all appearance had little reason to expect any considerable assistance from his freinds there, if held in the same light with those in Northumberland, where only two gentlemen joined him, yet he was determined that they should not have it to say that it was oweing to the difficulty of passing the militia in the Country, and that their people were unwilling to rise without some troops to make a head for them, and therefore fixed his departure for the 20th. To have laid there [i.e. at Carlisle] any longer would have been both idle and dangerous....Mr Wade [being] at Newcastle, and the 2 Regiments with the foot detached to Scotland on his left. So, to prevent a junction of the D[uke of Cumberland's] and Mr Wade's armies, his only proper methode was to march forward, that in case he came to action he might only have one army to deal with, whereas had they Continued [at Carlisle] till the D[uke of Cumberland']s march north, who would have been joined by Mr Wade from Newcastle...he had only 3 things to choose upon – first, to fight with an army more than 3 times his number, give them the Slip if possible, and march South, where it was most certain nobody would join him, seeing such a powerfull army in his rear.... Or lastly to have retired to Scottland." [16]

In fact Wade had already made a half-hearted advance towards the Jacobite army, but hearing on 17th November that Carlisle had already fallen and faced with a difficult passage over the Pennines through the snow-bound Tyne Gap, he retreated back to Newcastle and played no further significant role in the campaign.

The Jacobites, having left a small garrison at Carlisle, marched doggedly on over Lazonby Fell and down to Penrith arriving on 21st November where the Prince lodged at the George and Dragon Inn. On the following day they continued their march, in deep snow and a bitter wind, over Shap Fell and into the little market town of Kendal. A contemporary observer (no doubt a Whig!) wrote a vivid account of the state of the Jacobite army as they entered the town in a letter to the London Evening Post:-

"Should 2,000 of their best be drafted out of this brave army, the rest would be such a poor, lousy, miserable pack, that any man who did not know their errand, and if they had not arms, would imagine some great famine to be in Scotland, and that these poor creatures were come into England to beg their bread. They have several young men in close plaid waistcoats, and huge fur caps, which they call their hussars; but they have such scurvy horses, that I have seen several of them exert all their vigour to bring them to a gallop; in spite of which the poor beasts immediately fell into a pace more suitable to their age and infirmities." [17]

The Prince lodged for the nights of 23rd and 24th November at Stricklandgate House, and the next day marched on to Lancaster. By 26th November the army had reached Preston. Here, in traditionally royalist Lancashire, with a significant minority of Catholics, he could expect to pick up a substantial number of new recruits, but the results were extremely disappointing. The Prince himself received a tumultuous welcome, but the inhabitants seemed content to confine their support to cheers and flag-waving. Few of them were prepared to risk all by joining the Jacobite army. As O'Sullivan put it:-

"It can't be expressed wth what demonstrations of joy the Prince was rec'd here, bells ringing, bonfires, all the houses illuminated, such crouds of people, yt the guardes cou'd not keep them of; everey body, man and woman, must tutch him, & such a continual cry of "God blesse the King and the Prince" yt it was thought they wou'd all follow & bring him directly to London. A great many of them took party, but did not follow." [18]

However, the Prince did gain one useful recruit at Preston in the person of Francis Townley of Townley Hall. Townley was from a Catholic family and had formerly been in the service of the French army. He was a devoted Jacobite whose uncle Richard had joined the Jacobite forces in 1715. We shall hear more of him in due course. So disappointing were the results that, as the Chevalier Johnstone relates, one of his more enterprising recruiting sergeants decided to go on ahead to Manchester where it was thought that there might be better prospects of success:-

"I had enlisted one of my sergeants, named Dickson, from among the prisoners of war at Prestonpans. He was a young Scotsman, as brave and intrepid as a lion, and very much attached to my interest. On the 27th, at Preston, he informed me that he had been beating up for recruits all day without getting one, and that he was the more chagrined at this as the other sergeants had had better success. He therefore came to ask my permission to get a day's march ahead of the army by setting out immediately for Manchester...in order to make sure of some recruits before their arrival. I reproved him sharply for entertaining so wild and extravagant a project, which exposed him to the danger of being taken and hanged, and I ordered him back to his company.....On entering my quarters in the evening, my landlady informed me that my servant had called and taken away my portmanteau and blunderbuss. I immediately bethought myself of his extravagant project, and his situation gave me much uneasiness. But on our arrival in Manchester, on the evening of the following day... Dickson brought me about one hundred and eighty recruits, whom he had enlisted for my company. He had quitted Preston, in the evening, with his mistress and my drummer. Having marched all night he arrived next morning at Manchester, which is about thirty miles distant from Preston, and immediately began to beat up for recruits for "the yellow haired laddie" [i.e. Prince Charles]. The populace, at first, did not interrupt him, conceiving our army to be near the town; but as soon as they knew it would not arrive till the evening, they surrounded him in a tumultuous manner, with the intention of taking him prisoner, alive or dead. Dickson presented his blunderbuss, which was charged with slugs, and threatened to blow out the brains of those who first dared to lay hands on himself or the two who accompanied him. By turning round continually, facing in all directions and behaving like a lion, he soon enlarged the circle which a crowd of people had formed round them. Having continued for some time to manoeuvre in this way, those of the inhabitants of Manchester who were attached to the house of Stuart, took arms and flew to the assistance of Dickson, to rescue him from the fury of the mob, so that he soon had five or six hundred men to aid him, who dispersed the crowd in a very short time. Dickson now triumphed in his turn, and putting himself at the head of his followers, he proudly paraded, undisturbed, the whole day, with his drummer, enlisting for my company all who offered themselves." [19]

At Garstang there had been another small encouragement for the Prince when a local gentleman, John Daniel, was persuaded by the Duke of Perth, to join the army, and the Jacobites managed to gain a further 38 recruits. This is his account of his initiation into the Jacobite army:-

"The brave and illustrious Duke of Perth... halting to refresh himself at a Public-House upon the road, where with some friends of mine I happened to be; His Grace, being truly zealous in the cause, asked of them the disposition of the place and people. They replied, that they believed it to be much in the Prince's favour. After some conversation on one thing and another, the Duke did me the honour to invite me to join; which request being nowise contrary to my inclination, I immediately answered His Grace, that I was exceeding willing to do anything that lay in my power for promoting the Prince's interests....Upon this the Duke honoured me with a most sincere promise of his particular patronage; and not a little proud I was of acquiring such a friend on my first joining the Prince's army....After some questions, the Duke desired me to get in readiness and to meet him on horseback at Garstang; which in about two or three hours I accordingly did." [20]

The highland army left Preston on 28th November, spent that night in Wigan, and on 29th November entered the important and populous town of Manchester. The Prince himself arrived at about 2 p.m. and lodged at a house in Market Street. Lord Elcho describes their reception:-

"...when the Prince arrived with his army at Manchester, the Mob huzza'd him to his Lodgings, the town was mostly illuminated, and the Bells rung. Their were several substantial people came and kis'd his hand, and a vast number of people of all sorts came to see him supp." [21]

The entry of the Jacobites was also recorded by Elizabeth (known to her family as "Beppy") Byrom, an enthusiastic supporter of the Prince, who lived at a house in the Market Place, now the Old Wellington Inn adjacent to Harvey Nichols Department Store:-

"...eleven o'clock we went up to the Cross to see the rest come in; there came small parties of them till about three o'clock, when the Prince and the main body of them came, I cannot guess how many. The Prince went straight up to Mr Dickenson's, where he lodges...There came an officer up to us at [the] Cross and gave us the manifests and declarations; the bells they rung, and P Cotterel made a bonfire, and all the town was illuminated, every house except Mr Dickenson's, my papa, mamma and sister, and my uncle and I walked up and down to see it; about four o'clock the King was proclaimed, the mob shouted very cleverly, and then we went up to see my aunt Brearcliffe and stayed till eleven o'clock making St Andrew's crosses for them." [22]

The occupation of Manchester, without a blow being struck, brought home the threat to the midland counties, and Derbyshire in particular, in a way that nothing else could have done. There had always been close social and economic ties between Manchester and the north west of Derbyshire. James Clegg's sons lived and worked in Manchester, and he was a frequent visitor there. His diary entries at this time sound an increasing note of alarm and desperation:-

"25/11/45 – We hear the Rebels are advancing fast towards Manchester and the people are removing and concealing their best effects

26//11/45 – At home till noon then was called up to Chappell to dine with Mr Butterworth and two of Mr Baily's sons and their wives, who are flying for safety to Sheffield. At night I sent away my wife's cloathes and Linnen and some writings to be concealed a while

27/11/45 – We hear some of the Rebels are come into Manchester, our town is full of Refugees…

28/11/45 - ….all the news is discouraging, Stockport Bridge is broke down but we know not which way the Rebels intend to go from Manchester

29/11/45 – I walked up to town in the morning to see my friends and hear tidings, all are full of fears, May God appear for our defence". [23]

Manchester was at this time a town with a large number of Tory and Jacobite sympathizers, and a strong and militant body of non-juring clergy. These were the Anglicans who had refused to take the Oath of Allegiance to William in 1688 and continued to form their own separate congregations. At last it must have seemed to the Jacobites that they were entering friendly territory where they could expect to raise substantial numbers of recruits for the army. Certainly they did better in Manchester than they had along the way from Scotland, but the success was relative. According to the Jacobite Quartermaster, John William O'Sullivan, they had expected to raise some 1,500 men. In fact they managed to raise about two to three hundred recruits, partly from the large population of under-employed weavers. Many of the new recruits were from other parts of Lancashire, and we can only be sure that about 25 were from the city itself. These became the Manchester Regiment, were attired in blue serge coats and a tartan sash and placed under the command of Francis Townley. There were also other recruits, somewhat higher up the social scale; one was the Rev Thomas Coppock, son of a Manchester tailor who was a prominent non-juring Anglican clergyman and became the Regimental Chaplain of the Manchester Regiment. He would march with the army to Derby.

Even though the addition of a further three hundred or so recruits was welcome to the depleted Jacobite army, up to one thousand of whom may have deserted on the march south, the active support of Jacobite sympathizers in England so far had been extremely disappointing, and far less than the Prince and his senior officers might have hoped for and, indeed, expected from the reports of Jacobite agents before the rising commenced. There must, by now, have been grave doubts about whether the march into England could continue. On the evening of 29th November, at the Prince's lodgings in Market Street, there was another council of war, recorded by Lord Elcho in his journal in which the dilemma of the Jacobite army is succinctly set out:-

"The Prince was so far deceaved with these proceedings of bonfires and ringing of bells... that he thought himself sure of Success, and his Conversation that night at Table was, in what manner he should enter London, on horseback or afoot, and in what dress...The Principall officers of the army, who thought otherwise upon these topics, mett at Manchester and were of Opinion that now they had marched far enough into England, and as they had received not the least Encouragement from any person of distinction, the French not landed, and only joined by 200 vagabonds, they had done their part; and as they did not pretend to put a King upon the throne of England without their consent, that it was time to represent to the Prince to go back to Scotland. But after talking a great deal about it, it was determin'd to march to Derby, so that neither the French nor the English might have it to Say, the army had not marched far Enough into England to give the one Encouragement to Land and the other to join." [24]

Accordingly the highland army left Manchester on Monday 1st December and marched to Macclesfield. Their arrival was described in a letter by a local Attorney, John Stafford:-

"After about four or five Regiments had passed by us it was said that the P[rince] was coming up. You may safely imagine we were all very attentive to see him, and it happened a halt was made just outside my Door for a minute or two which gave us an opportunity of having a very full View of him; He was in Highland dress...with a blue Highland cap on, and was surrounded by about 40 who appeared to be his Guard. He is a very hansome person of a man rather tall, exactly proportioned and walks very well....I believe they made their best appearance into the town expecting to be received as they were at

Manchester, But there was profound silence and nothing to be seen on ye countenances of ye Inhabitants but horror and amazement." [25]

At Macclesfield it became clear to the Jacobites that the Duke of Cumberland, formerly in command of the army in Flanders, but now hurriedly recalled to take over command of the government forces in the Midlands from Sir John Ligonier, was massing his troops in Staffordshire in order to bar the road to London. The Duke was a younger son of King George, was aged 25 at the time (the same age as the Prince), and was a professional army officer with two campaigns in Flanders behind him. In order to avoid the government forces, a stratagem was therefore suggested by Lord George Murray:-

"...We had certain intelligence that the Duke of Cumberland's army was on its march, and were quartered at Litchfield [sic], Coventry, Stafford, and Newcastle under Line [sic]. We resolved to march for Derby; and to cover our intentions, I offered to go with a column of the army to Congleton, which was the straight road to Litchfield, so that the enemy would have reason to think we intended to come upon them, which would make them gather in a body, and readily advance upon that road, so that we could get before them to Derby." [26]

This feint succeeded beyond all expectations. As Lord George Murray approached with his column, an outpost of the Duke of Kingston's light horse retired from Newcastle-under-Lyme to Lichfield, leaving behind the Hanoverian spy Vere (or Weir) who was captured in his underclothes in a local public house. Cumberland, fearing that the direction of the Jacobites' march demonstrated an intention to invade Wales, where they were believed to have strong support, moved his troops from Lichfield northwest to Stone. Having thus decoyed the government troops so far west that they could no longer bar the London road, Lord George turned eastwards towards Rushton Spencer and joined the Prince with the rest of the army just outside Leek which the combined army reached on the evening of 3rd December. The Prince's army was now poised to invade Derbyshire and the main road from Derby to London lay open and undefended.

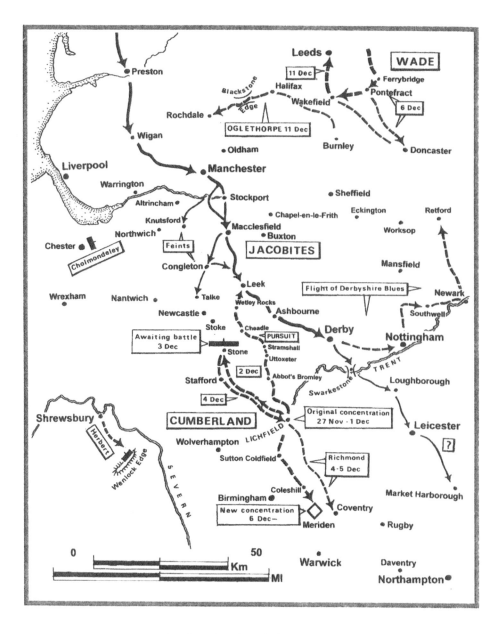

2. Cumberland deceived

Chapter 4

Derby and Derbyshire in 1745

A mid-eighteenth century map of Derbyshire shows the boundaries of the county then to have been very much as they are now – a long, roughly triangular shape, broader at the top than the bottom, and divided administratively into a number of "hundreds"- High Peak, Scarsdale and Wirksworth in the north and east, Appletree, Morelton & Litchurch and Repton & Gresley in the south and west. Topographically, too the terrain was then very similar, bleak open moorland in the High Peak, very much more remote then than now, notwithstanding the recent opening of the turnpike from Derby to Sheffield, and largely devoted to sheep grazing, with most of the county's cultivated arable land in the south on the fertile soils of the Trent and Derwent valleys.

The county's main industry was still the ancient one of lead mining, centred mainly in the Middle and High Peak, particularly around Wirksworth and Matlock. The Romans had mined lead here 1,500 years before, and although the industry had declined somewhat from its heyday at the end of the 17th century, it still employed very large numbers of people. Some twenty years earlier, Daniel Defoe had published his impression of Wirksworth and its inhabitants, at the heart of the lead-mining industry, in his book "A Tour Through the Whole Island of Great Britain" published between 1724 and 1727:-

"It is a large well-frequented market town, and market towns being very thin placed in this part of the county, they have the better trade, the people generally coming twelve or fifteen miles to a market, and sometimes much more; though there is no very great trade to this town but what relates to the lead works and to the subterranean wretches, who they call Peakrills, who work in the mines and who live all round this town every way. The inhabitants are a rude boorish kind of people, but they are a bold, daring and even desperate kind of fellows in their search into the Bowels of the Earth; for no people in the world outdo them; and therefore they are often entertained by our Engineers in the Wars to carry on the Sap [i.e. mining], and other such works, at the Siege of strong fortified places." [27]

The other main industries in the county were coal mining, and iron ore mining, both centred, at this time, mainly in and around

Alfreton and the north east of the county. Coal mining was normally carried out from surface mines, what we now call open-cast mining, resulting in many small individual pits. Iron ore mining from the local ironstone in the same area was done in the same fashion and smelted locally.

Most of the county, however, was still agricultural, especially the south western part, Appletree Hundred, through which the Jacobite army would march on its way to Derby. This was the arable and stock raising area which supplied the beasts for Derby's monthly cattle and horse fair. As in the rest of England most of the land was owned by the landed gentry whose names would have been familiar to the protagonists of the civil war 100 years earlier - the Poles, Everys, Curzons, Harpurs and Mundays, all the traditional leaders of society that made up the great and the good and provided the Lords Lieutenant, High Sheriffs and Magistracy on which the administration of the county depended.

Transport in the county was difficult. Most of the roads were not yet turnpiked and were generally in a poor or, at best, indifferent state of repair. The main north south route was the Sheffield to Derby road which ran through Chesterfield and Duffield to Derby. This was notoriously bad with many steep hills and declivities making the transport of heavy wagons difficult at the best of times and next to impossible in bad weather. There had been a turnpike act passed in 1739 for the Bakewell to Chesterfield and Worksop road, but it was more honoured in the breach than the observance and little effort was made to keep it in good repair. In theory, each parish was supposed to put part of its rates to use in keeping its section of the turnpike in good repair, but in areas with a small and thinly spread population this often proved impossible. Parishes which failed in this duty were prosecuted at the Quarter Sessions and there are numerous instances of this happening in Derbyshire at the time. For example, Brampton was presented at the Quarter Sessions in 1749 for failing to keep in repair its section of the Bakewell to Chesterfield road, and Somercotes was indicted in 1738 and again in 1746 for dereliction of repairs on the Alfreton to Nottingham road.

Much transport relied, therefore, on the rivers (there were no canals in the county at this date) particularly the navigable sections of the Trent and the Derwent which were used to ship the county's main industrial products of iron, coal and lead to its entrepot at Hull. This gave the rivers, and especially their bridges, great strategic importance. On the Trent, the ancient bridge at Swarkestone was the last bridgeable crossing of the river; thereafter it widened to a breadth that made bridging impossible and any crossing of the river further downstream depended on a ferry. The Trent, in its lower reaches, was a significant barrier to travel between the midland and northern counties. All of these difficulties, however, would be brushed aside by the hard marching highland army.

Derby itself, the county town, was a small but busy and enterprising place. We have no precise figures for its population in 1745. However, in 1712 it was estimated at 4,000 and in 1788 it was about 8,500, so a median figure of perhaps 6,000 is probably about right. It was described in the letterpress of a map published in 1728 as "a rich and populous town delightfully situate on the Brink of the River Darewent, which is lately made navigable into the Trent. Besides many other stately buildings, the noble and lofty Tower of All Saint's Church is a grand ornament to this Town, the body of which hath in a very beautiful manner lately been rebuilt. Likewise the Silk Mills so famous for their works, and wherein a great number of people are employ'd are great additions to the beauty of this prospect."

All Saint's Church, which would figure so largely in the Jacobite occupation of Derby, had been built in the 14th Century and replaced a much earlier church. Its most prominent feature was its magnificent Gothic spire built between 1510 and 1530. In 1725 its vicar, the Reverend Mitchell Hutchinson, irritated by the refusal of the corporation to sanction much needed repairs to the nave, paid some workmen to demolish it secretly one night thus presenting the authorities with a fait accompli. The nave was rebuilt to the design of the architect James Gibbs in 1725. In 1730 a fine wrought iron rood screen by Robert Bakewell was installed, at a cost of £157.10.0d and in 1740 the church (not then a cathedral, of course) received its first organ, bought second-hand. The tower still had its original 16th Century carillon which, in the eighteenth century played the following tunes:-

Sunday – Hanover
Monday – Lass of Pattie's Mill
Tuesday – Highland Laddie
Wednesday – Shady Bowers
Thursday – National Anthem
Friday – Handel's March from Scipio
Saturday – Silken Garter

The Sunday and Tuesday choices are particularly resonant in view of the events of December 1745. Adjacent to the church was Derby's oldest public house the half-timbered Dolphin Inn, built in 1530. Other notable churches were St Werburgh's at the bottom of Sadler Gate, where Dr Johnson had been married to his much older wife Elizabeth "Tetty" Porter in 1735, St Alkmund's on the road from Derby to Duffield and, south east of the Market Place, St Peter's on St Peter's Street. [28]

The other outstanding building in Derby was the Silk Mill. At the end of the 17th Century a local barrister, Thomas Cotchett (his father Robert had been an eyewitness of the execution of King Charles in 1649) introduced silk-spinning to Derby, building a mill on the island in the Derwent known as The Holmes to the design of the engineer George Sorocold who had recently built the waterworks at St Michael's which supplied the town with clean water. It was 62 feet long and 28 feet wide, had three stories and employed Dutch silk spinning machines with a total of 1,340 spindles and 8,410 bobbins. It was the wonder of its age. In 1717, one of the apprentices at the mill, John Lombe, hearing that the Italian silk spinning machines were much better than the Dutch, went to work in Italy, memorized all the workings of the Italian machines, and brought the designs back to Derby. He took over Cotchett's mill and built a new one in 1721. Sorocold made the new Italian style machines and within a few years the mill had 26 winding machines to wind the silk thread from the cocoons with 12,600 spindles, a spinning machine and 143 doubling mills which twisted the fine silk into usable silk thread. When John Lombe died in 1729 his brother Robert took over the business, was eventually knighted and received a grant from the government of £14,000 (an enormous sum in those days) for his services to the country. By 1745 the mill employed several hundred people and was probably the biggest employer in Derby. [29]

As well as the silk industry, Derby and mid-Derbyshire were also famous for their stocking frame workers. The stocking frame, a mechanical device for knitting stockings and operated manually, had been invented by a Nottinghamshire clergyman in the late 16th Century, and by 1745 the stocking manufacturing business was widespread in the East Midlands, particularly in Nottinghamshire, Derbyshire and Leicestershire. Stocking frame knitters were self-employed home workers, who often rented their frames from richer industrialists, and their work was sporadic and uncertain; many were under-employed and one of the few recruits to the Jacobite army in Derby would be a stockinger.

Derby had many other fine public buildings apart from its churches and the Silk Mill. A new stone Guildhall had been built in the Market Place in 1730 to replace the old half-timbered one. This was where the aldermen and burgesses of the town council met. This stood at right angles to the famous Piazzas, built in 1708 as a colonnaded shopping area, behind which was The Shambles, the town butchery, and behind that Rotten Row, in the present day Cornmarket, which led up to Irongate. Also in the Market Place were a water pump and the Market Cross. On Full Street, adjacent to the Market Place, were the Assembly Rooms, built in 1714, and used for balls, routs and other public entertainments.

The wealthier members of society tended to live in and around the centre of town, in St Mary's Gate, where many of the larger town houses of the gentry and merchants could be found, and in Irongate and the Market Place. In 1745 the town had not yet begun to spread itself along the Wardwick and Friargate. The poorer members of society clustered in Nun's Green next to the Markeaton Brook, where there were many small manufactures and home industries.

In 1712 a Mr Woolley wrote a description of the town that would certainly have applied thirty years later:-

"It is at present a very large, populous, rich and well frequented Borough town, few inland towns in the kingdom equalling it, having above 700 free burgesses. It has five parish Churches, being in length from the top of St Peter's Parish in the South to Lodge Lane at the far end of St Hellen's in the North, about a mile, and from the upper end of the Friar Gate in St Werburgh's in the west to the Castle Hill in the East, near three-quarters of a mile. Though not very regularly built, yet it has a great many very good houses, especially on all parts of the outside of the town, mostly of brick, of which there are as good made in this town, and as cheap as in almost any part of England. It has many persons of good Quality, and a great number of coaches kept in it, has a very handsome Market Place, a square with good buildings about it." [30]

In spite of its small population, Derby appears to have been a busy, enterprising and lively town. It had a variety of clubs and societies; there was a Masonic Lodge, first established in 1732 and which met at the Virgin's Inn on the corner of the Market Place and Full Street. There was also a Society to Relieve the Widows of Clergymen, a Horticulturalist's Society and a Society of Musicians. The first newspaper, the Derby Postman, appeared in 1717, and was later joined by the Derby Mercury in 1732. The Mercury would be most active in reporting on the Jacobite occupation of Derby in December of 1745.

Most of the people of Derby and Derbyshire adhered to the Church of England, but there was also a small but influential body of dissenters, many of whom, Quakers in particular, were hard-working, sober, thrifty and enterprising. There was a long history of Quakerism in Derby – the founder of the sect, George Fox, had been imprisoned in Derby ninety years before for interrupting the vicar of All Saints during his sermon. In the county, particularly in the High Peak, there was a substantial number of Catholics, especially in and around Hathersage, where the local landed gentry, the Eyres, had maintained the faith since Elizabethan times. As always in times of civil disorder, the Catholics were viewed with suspicion by the authorities and were to be the subject of unwelcome attention in the days to come.

Chapter 5

Whigs and Tories

As labels indicating political affiliation, the terms "Whig" and "Tory" first came into general use at the time of the Exclusion Crisis of 1679. It was known that Charles II's brother, James, had converted to Roman Catholicism. Charles had no legitimate heirs and there was widespread concern that the Catholic James would ultimately inherit the throne and impose a "Divine Right" Catholic autocracy on Britain's unwilling Protestant population. An Exclusion Bill was therefore presented to Parliament the purpose of which was to exclude James from the succession. The proponents of the bill were known at that time as the "country party" but were very soon referred to by their opponents as "Whiggamores", a reference to a party of Scots Rebels of that name who marched to Edinburgh in 1648 in opposition to Charles I. This was soon shortened to Whig and denoted those supporters of the supremacy of Parliament over the monarchy who were the inheritors of the Parliamentarian position from the days of the Civil Wars. The Whigs retaliated by referring to their opponents as Tories, derived from the Irish word for an outlaw "toraidhe" - this had been used as a term of abuse to refer to Irish Royalist rebels during the Civil War, particularly those Irish soldiers whom Charles I wished to bring over to England in 1644 in order to buttress his declining forces. By the time of the "Glorious Revolution" Whig and Tory had come to mean respectively, the supporters of the Hanoverian succession and their opponents, those who had adopted the mantle of the Cavaliers of the Civil War and who tended to favour the Crown as against Parliament; they were often Anglicans of a high church persuasion, and by the time of the 1745 rising many of them were non-jurors (see infra). These two parties, hardly deserving of the term by comparison with present-day politics, were loose and often changing alliances of those with political power and influence in the country, but after the deposition of James II, the Whig party, as one would expect, dominated British politics for the next seventy years. That did not mean, however, that the Tories were prepared to roll over and put their paws in the air - on the contrary many elections to Parliament were bitterly contested, often divisive, and frequently accompanied by allegations of corruption and the threat of violence.

In Derby and Derbyshire, the politics of the town and county were complicated and occasionally turbulent. In 1637 Derby had obtained a new charter from Charles I which provided for a town council consisting of a mayor, ten aldermen, fourteen brethren and fourteen common councillors. Derby also elected two MP's, the electors being the freemen of the borough. In 1700 there were 532 freemen eligible to vote, perhaps 40% of the adult male suffrage at the time. The county of Derbyshire elected a further two MP's.

What level of political support could Prince Charles expect as he marched his army into Derbyshire along the road from Leek? In November 1743 the Jacobite agent James Butler wrote a lengthy report for Louis XV of France on the strength of Jacobite support in England. It was headed "Circumstances of the lords and gentry of highest reputation in the various counties of England, who may be counted upon" and listed those who would be likely to come out in support of a Jacobite rising. It proved to be wildly optimistic. It was based on the wholly incorrect assumption that all Tory supporters were also Jacobites, and this is what it had to say about Derbyshire:-

"Derbyshire – The Duke of Rutland and Lord Chesterfield [a leading minister in the government], Sir Nathaniel Curzon and Mr John Stanhope dominate the whole county; Sir Nathaniel Curzon, who has a rental of £12,000, has 10,000 miners at his command." [31]

Not only does this give a very misleading impression of Jacobite support in the county, but it also leaves out of account completely the enormous influence and power of Whig magnates such as the Duke of Devonshire, whose network of friends, family and supporters was spread much more widely in the county than simply his family estates at Chatsworth. His example in opposing the insurgents would be vital in deterring other members of the gentry in Derbyshire from expressing open support for the Prince.

A closer look at the history of parliamentary elections in Derby and Derbyshire will give much insight into the extent of local support for the Jacobite cause. In Derby in 1710 and 1713 two Tory MP's were returned for the town, and in 1715 they were "only defeated after an orgy of bribery and intimidation which led to an [election] petition, afterwards withdrawn." The impeachment of the Tory and pro-Jacobite Anglican divine Dr Henry Sacheverall, partly owing to a seditious sermon preached at All Saints in August 1709 resulted in his conviction, but he received only a nominal sentence. This was greeted with acclamation in Derby "the bells of All Saints clashed out a triumphant peal, which was shortly taken up by every steeple in the town, while huge bonfires were piled up and set on fire in the centre of the Market Place and on Nun's Green".

The General Election of 1710 had seen a resurgence of support for the Tories and a landslide of Tory MP's. The death of Queen Anne, however, meant the succession of the House of Hanover, minor German princelings with little interest in Britain and with whom many Britons failed to identify. The coronation of George I in 1714 caused riots in many parts of the country, including Derby, where a mob gathered, windows were broken and local notables who were Whig supporters were openly insulted in the streets. Hutton, in his History of Derby, neatly summarises the exhibition of Jacobite sentiment amongst the Derby clergy at this time:-

"Sturges of All Saints prayed publicly for King James but after a moment [said] "I mean King George". The congregation became tumultuous; the military gentlemen drew their swords and ordered him out of the pulpit into which he never returned. He pleaded a slip of the tongue; but if he had dipped into the New Testament, he might have sheltered himself under a better excuse, for we are there commanded to pray for our enemies. Harris of St Peter's was repeatedly called to order by the powerful voice of the magistrates. Cantril, of St Alkmund's, drank the Pretender's health upon his knees, and the Thirtieth of January became the most holy day in the year." [this was the day which commemorated the death of King Charles I, a martyr to all loyal Anglicans] [32]

After the failure of the risings of 1715 (in which a local clergyman, the Reverend Buxton took part as one of the chaplains to the Jacobite army), and 1719, the government was dominated for the next thirty years by the Whigs, who were committed supporters of the Hanoverian dynasty. Derby and Derbyshire, like most of the country south of the border, remained quiescent, but the abandonment by the government of an unpopular excise bill in 1733 gave rise to country-wide demonstrations of anti-Hanoverian sentiment. A general election followed in 1734. In Derbyshire there was a bruising contest between the Tory candidate, and avowed Jacobite, Sir Nathaniel Curzon, and the Whig magnate, and youngest son of the 2nd Duke of Devonshire, Lord Charles Cavendish. Derbyshire was virtually a family seat of the Devonshires, and Cavendish won but only by a narrow margin. The outcome, which was generally believed to have been rigged, resulted in serious disturbances in Derby by a pro-Tory mob. In Derby itself the Whig candidates, Lord James Cavendish, another son of the Duke, and the Honourable Charles Stanhope, son of the Earl of Chesterfield, also won by a very narrow margin of 59 votes.

In 1742 there was a by-election in Derby, one of the sitting MP's having been elevated to office in the government. Another very close result ensued. The Tory candidate was German Pole of Radbourne Hall (of whom more later), considered by Eardley-Simpson to have been a Jacobite supporter. Whether he was or not is a matter of controversy, but at all events he ran the Whig candidate a very close second. The Whig was Viscount Duncannon, a son in law of the Duke of Devonshire. In a vote which was clearly rigged by the Whig mayor of Derby, Samuel Fox, German Pole lost by only 46 votes out of a total electorate of 646. An election petition was subsequently lodged but, as in 1715, was subsequently withdrawn. Voting was not then done by means of a secret ballot and the voting choice of all the electors was a matter of public record. It is clear from the Poll Book that the Tory vote came mainly from the "lower orders" – frame-work knitters, butchers, tailors, brick-makers, wool-combers, blacksmiths and tanners all voted for Pole. The Whig support, by contrast, came from the upper echelons of society in the town, from merchants, lawyers, aldermen, and even a Presbyterian preacher, all of those groups who had prospered under the Hanoverians and therefore had most to lose from the downfall of the Whig oligarchy. Judging by the result of the 1742 election, therefore, the most recent opportunity for people to express their political affiliations, the Jacobites could expect to draw their support from the poorer labouring classes rather than the wealthy tradesmen and professional classes of Derby. This, however, pre-supposes that support for the Tory party meant support for the restoration of the Stuarts; that this was not necessarily so rapidly became apparent as the highlanders marched into Derby on 4th December 1745.

An important indication of Jacobite support was the presence, or otherwise, of the so-called "Jacobite Drinking Club". There were many of these and Jacobite coffee houses during the first half of the 18th Century. Some, clearly social rather than political, openly displayed their sympathies, others were clandestine, and we know little of them, but they were likely to have been the more active politically and were no doubt the haunt of Jacobite agents. There is little doubt, however, that their memberships overlapped from time to time. The most famous of the social drinking clubs was the Cocoa Tree in St James's, London. There were others in London: the Oak Society, which met at the Crown and Anchor Inn in the Strand, the Beaufort Club which met at Truby's, and the Board of Brothers which met at various London taverns. In the provinces there were many more drinking clubs and also a number of Jacobite hunts which met regularly. No records have yet been found of Jacobite clubs in Derbyshire, but it would be surprising if there were not at least one where Jacobite sympathizers could toast "the little gentleman in the black velvet waistcoat" and raise their glasses "to the King over the water". In Congleton, only 25 miles from Derby, there was a Jacobite hunt which met regularly and in Manchester a Jacobite society called John Shaw's Club had been founded in 1738. The Cheshire Club was even earlier. Having been founded in 1689, it held its meetings at Lyme Hall, the home of Peter Legh of Lyme. It had dissolved in about 1720, but re-formed in 1745 and apparently decided by one vote not to join the highlanders in their march south. The adjoining county of Staffordshire was a well-known hotbed of Jacobite activity, so the Prince might reasonably expect a substantial flow of recruits and supporters to join him in Derbyshire, if not a flood.

Another aspect of covert Jacobite activity was the Jacobite Masonic lodge. This too is still a subject of controversy and would benefit from much more historical research. There seems to be little if any agreement about whether or not there was a strong connection between masonry and the Jacobite cause. Some historians have asserted that the "Ancient and Accepted Scottish Rite", which had first appeared with the establishment of the Canongate Killiwinning Lodge in Edinburgh, was itself a secret expression of Jacobite sympathies, and have asserted that Prince Charles himself was inducted into the brotherhood in Rome. Others assert that there is little, if any, connection between the Stuarts and the Jacobite cause and Freemasonry. There is, however, one tantalising morsel of information concerning Freemasonry in Derbyshire. It is alleged that the warrant for the establishment of the Masonic lodge based at Longnor in 1745 was signed by Bonnie Prince Charlie while he was in Derby. Alas the original warrant is no longer extant, but it is interesting to speculate that the Prince might have found the time whilst in Derby to concern himself with Masonic matters. Personally I have some doubts. He was, I suspect, far too busy trying to drum up support locally and arguing with his senior commanders to concern himself with the affairs of the local lodge.

After the rising was over, there was a riot in Lichfield in 1747, which was supposedly the work of clandestine Jacobite supporters (there is a famous print of it that was published at the time), and which is sometimes adduced as evidence of continuing support for the Stuart dynasty in the Midlands. However, looking at the course of Derby and Derbyshire's politics over the thirty years prior to the rising, perhaps the most we can say is that there was a substantial amount of support for the Tory party, but this did not necessarily translate into support for the Jacobite cause - most Jacobites were Tories, but that does not mean to say that most Tories were Jacobites. Whatever their secret allegiance may have been, when push came to shove virtually no-one in Derby and its environs, whatever their social class, was prepared to elevate sympathy into action.

Chapter 6

The Jacobites Occupy Derby

The Prince's division of the army marched from Macclesfield at 4 a.m. on Tuesday 3rd December. In the vanguard was Pitsligo's Horse followed by Lord Ogilvie's Regiment; behind them came the Edinburgh Regiment of John Roy Stewart, the Duke of Perth's Regiment, a mixed contingent of highlanders and lowlanders plus some English volunteers and redcoat deserters from Cope's army captured at Prestonpans. Then came part of the artillery (the so-called "Swedish guns" landed from French privateers in October). Next in the line of march were the clan regiments of Cameron of Lochiel, Cluny MacPherson, MacDonald of Glengarry, and the MacDonalds of Keppoch, Clanranald and Glencoe. Last came the rest of the artillery, including the small Coehorn mortar, guarded by the Stewarts of the Appin Regiment and the rearguard consisting of Gordon of Glenbucket's Regiment and the remainder of Pitsligo's Horse. Guarding the baggage train was the newly recruited Manchester Regiment. By 11 o'clock that morning the advance guard had entered the little village of Whide and by 6 p.m. the whole of the Prince's division had arrived in Leek.

The local population was hostile to the Jacobite cause and went to considerable trouble to avoid the inevitable seizure of food, fodder and horses. Farms at Swytherley and Heaton concealed their cattle in a ravine, and a local magistrate, William Marshall, was taken hostage in reprisal and had to pay £300 for his release. Overnight the Prince lodged in the home of Mr Mills on the Market Place while his men prepared for all eventualities by sharpening their dirks and broadswords on the ancient Norman cross in the churchyard. Only one recruit joined the army at Leek, a man named Goole from the nearby village of Wanlow.

In the meantime, Lord George Murray's division had marched from Congleton before dawn and reached Leek at about 9 a.m. Pausing for a short while they then marched on to Ashbourne reaching the town about 3 p.m. where they halted for the night, Lord George probably staying at Ashbourne Hall. There is a local legend that the Prince also stayed there, but this seems unlikely – there is no other evidence to support it and the order book of the Jacobite army makes it clear that the Prince's division spent the night at Leek.

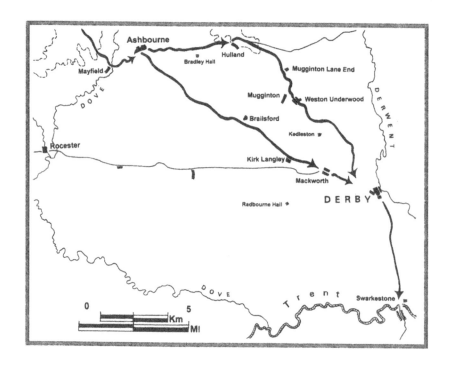

3. The March through Derbyshire

The Prince's sojourn at Leek was a short one. At 1 a.m. on Wednesday 4th December his division left the town and marched to Ashbourne where they arrived at dawn to join up with Lord George Murray's division. In Ashbourne King James III was proclaimed in the Market Place where the population seems to have been much more sympathetic than the Whig inhabitants of Leek. Ashbourne had had an active congregation of non-jurors since at least 1741 which met at Compton under the leadership of Thomas Bedford, a non-juring bishop, and the chaplain to the Jacobite baronet Sir Robert Cotton of Huntingdon. The highland army was met by crowds lining the streets, many of them wearing the white cockade denoting Jacobite supporters and shouting acclamations.

From Ashbourne the army continued on to Derby. Two Jacobite quartermasters reached the town at 11 a.m. and demanded quarters for what they said was an army of 9,000 men. It was a familiar ruse by the Jacobites during their invasion of England to inflate their numbers in order to deceive the enemy. In fact, at this stage in their march south the Prince's army probably numbered no more than about 5,500 men. The rest of the army followed on behind, split once again into two divisions, Lord George Murray's division marching directly from Ashbourne to Derby via Mackworth, roughly along the line of the present A52, and the Prince's division by the back roads via Bradley, Hulland Ward, Mugginton, Weston Underwood and Kedleston. One of the officers in Lord George Murray's division was John MacLean, a professional soldier who had started his career in the government's "Black Watch" highland companies in 1726. At this time he was a captain in the combined regiment of MacLachlans, and MacLeans which formed part of Nairne's Regiment of the Atholl Brigade. He kept a journal during the campaign and described the army's march through the little village of Mackworth as they approached Derby:-

"Wednesday the 4 Decembr we marched from Ashburn [Ashbourne] and passed through Brilsford [Brailsford] a Countrey Long Town and at severall houses we saw White flags hanging out Such as Napkins and white Aprons, and in the Gavels of Some houses white Cockades fixed. And after that we passed ane other town Called Mackwith [Mackworth] and They had a Bonefire in the Middle of the Town, and as oft as a Captain of a Company passed by the Whole Croud of the town who were gathered about that fire Gave a huza and the men waving their hats. And as we were out of the Town a Jolly hearty man mett us who wished us good Success and Said we should see him the Morrow with five hundred not one among them worse than himself". [33]

This "jolly hearty man" was a local framework knitter called James Sparkes, or Sparks, one of only five men to join the Prince's army at Derby. He was apparently something of a local rogue – he is mentioned in a contemporary letter by Dr Mather who wrote "They listed Sparks… at Derby, but sent him back from Ashburn [on the retreat] as too great a rogue to keep with them. He fell to plundering at Bradley, so He will probably be hang'd". [34]

As the Prince's division marched across country to Derby, they stopped on the way at Bradley Hall, near Ashbourne. Here they met with the local Squire, Littleton Poyntz Meynell, an eccentric and reputedly a Jacobite supporter. He had buried his silver plate in the garden on the approach of the army, but provided the Prince and his entourage with refreshment. One of the highlanders presented Meynell with his highland targe [shield] when he was billeted at the Meynell's town house in Derby, and it remains in the possession of the family to this day.

James Clegg, the assiduous diarist from Chapel en le Frith, noted the onward march of the highland army in his entry for 4th December 1745:-

"Very early I sent my man to Derby with letters for son Ben but he could not meet with him. He left the letters and made hast out and saw the Rebels marching very near to Derby as he came and his mare narrowly escap'd being pressed for the use of the Rebels, he came back in good time at night having travelled about 54 miles that day" [35]

The exact route of the army into Derby remains unclear. It is suggested by Eardley Simpson that they followed the Ashbourne Road to Friar Gate, past Nun's Green, where the Jacobite artillery was parked, and hence into Irongate and past the George Inn to the Market Place. Christopher Duffy proposes a slightly different route – Friar Gate to Sadler Gate and thence to the Market Place. For troops marching from Ashbourne, entering Derby along Irongate would involve a substantial detour, either across Nun's Green, or across Markeaton Brook (not then culverted) and into Walker Lane. Perhaps the answer is that the Jacobite army, marching as it was in two separate divisions, entered the town by different routes: the Prince's division along Kedleston Road and Lord George Murray's along Ashbourne Road. From their separate entry points they may well have converged in the Market Place, the biggest open space in the town at the time, and the only one large enough to have accommodated 5,000 men in one place.

There is a detailed description of the Jacobite army's entry into Derby in the *Gentleman's Magazine* :-

"On Wednesday 4th December, about 11 o'clock, two of the rebels' vanguard entered the town, and at their entrance gave a specimen of what we were to expect of such villains, by seizing a very good horse belonging to young Mr Stanford, after which they rode up to The George, and there enquiring for the magistrates, demanded billets for 9,000 men or more. In a short time after the vanguard rode into town, consisting of about 30 men, clothed in blue, faced with red; most of them had on scarlet waistcoats with gold lace, and being likely men made a good appearance. They were drawn up in the market place, and sat on horse back 2 or 3 hours; at the same time the bells were rung and several bonfires made, to prevent any resentment of them that might ensue on our shewing a dislike of their coming among us. About 3 in the afternoon Lord Elcho, with the lifeguards, and many of their chiefs also arrived, on horseback, to the number of about 150, most of them clothed as above; these made a fine show, being the flower of their army: soon after their main body also marched into town, in tolerable order, six or eight abreast, with about eight standards, most of them white flags and a red cross. They had several bagpipers, who played as they marched along; they appeared in general to answer the description we have all along had of them, viz: most of their main body a parcel of shabby, lousy, pitiful-looked fellows, mixed up with old men and boys, dressed in dirty plaids and as dirty shirts, without breeches, and wore their stockings made of plaid not much above half way up their legs, and some without shoes, or neither one, and numbers of them so fatigued with their long march, that they really commanded our pity more than fear. Whilst the market place was filled with them, they ordered their pretended prince, before he arrived, to be publicly proclaimed, which was accordingly done by the common crier; they then insisted upon the magistrates appearing in their gowns, but being told they had sent them out of town, were content to have that ceremony excused. Their prince (as they called him) did not arrive until the dusk of the evening; he walked on foot, being attended with a great body of his men, who conducted him to his lodgings (the lord Exeter's) where he had guards placed all around the house." [36]

A letter from the Vicar of All Saints, Rev Henry Cantrell, gives further details of the proclamation of King James in Derby:-

"Before he (the prince) came into the town, Lord George Murray summon'd the Corporation to appear in their Habits before the Town Hall. Alderman Cooper appeared in his Furr Gown; Smith, Bakewell and Franceys were without, pretending they were not near at hand; the Gisbornes (Alderman John and Thomas and your old friend John) had left the Town as well as the Mayor. Lord George waiv'd the ceremony of the Habit, and only insisted that they should by their Cryer proclaim James the Third, King of England, Scotland, France and Ireland, which was done by the Cryer, the Town Clerk having likewise gone away." [37]

The reference to the Jacobite army's flags is interesting. Few of them have survived because those that were captured after the battle of Culloden in April 1746 were ordered to be burned by the public hangman in Edinburgh. However, we do know that the flag carried by the Manchester Regiment, for example, had the words "Liberty and Property" inscribed on one side and "Church and Country" on the other.

The Prince's Lifeguards carried a banner captured from Gardiner's Dragoons at the battle of Prestonpans; it was probably green in colour and bore the words "Britons Strike Home" on one side. It was carried by the Ensign of Balmerino's Troop, John Daniel, who had been recruited in Lancashire. Ogilvy's Regiment had a blue rectangular flag with a white saltire in the centre and the motto "Nemo Me Impune Lacessit" above ("no-one touches me with impunity" - the motto of Clan Chattan, as it happens).

The Prince's arrival on foot is typical of his leadership style as described by Lord Elcho:-

"Usually he wore the highland habit, and marched all the way to Derby on foot at the head of one of the columns. He never dined nor threw off his clothes at night, nor ate much at supper, but used to throw himself upon a bed at eleven o'clock and was up by four in the morning. As he had a prodigious strong constitution, he bore fatigue most surprisingly well." [38]

What then was the nature of the Jacobite army that had descended so unexpectedly on Derby? It is important to bear in mind that at this stage of the rising the Prince's army contained none of the French regular troops that would join him later in the campaign: the Irish Picquets of Lally's, Rooth's and Dillon's Regiments, the Royal Ecossais and Fitzjames's Horse, who did not arrive in Scotland until November of 1745. The army that occupied Derby was almost entirely a Scottish one, save for the Manchester Regiment, and the greater part of it consisted of Gaelic-speaking highland clansmen. Full details of the individual regiments can be found at Appendix 1 but the table below gives details of the numbers and composition of the Jacobite army as mustered at Edinburgh at the start of the invasion and which marched to Derby:-

CAVALRY

1st Troop Lord Elcho's Lifeguard	125
2nd Troop Balmerino's Horse	40
Horse Guards & Kenmure's Horse (Kilmarnock)	100
Pitsligo's Horse	120
Bagot's Hussars	70

INFANTRY

Cameron of Lochiel's regiment	740
Stewart of Ardshiel's Regiment (the Appin Regiment)	360
The Atholl Brigade (three regiments)	1000
MacDonald of Clanranald's Regiment	300
MacDonald of Keppoch's Regiment	400
MacDonald of Glencoe's Regiment	200
John Gordon of Glenbucket's Regiment	427
Lord Ogilvy's Regiment	500
Duke of Perth's Regiment	750
Robertson of Struan's Regiment	200
MacLachlan of MacLachlan's Regiment	260
MacGregor of Glencarnock's Regiment	300
Lord Nairn's Regiment	200
John Roy Stewart's Edinburgh Regiment	450
Various miscellaneous units (artillery, engineers etc)	100

GUNS

13 pieces of artillery, mainly 1½ pounders, and one small mortar. Some of these had been captured from Cope's army after the Battle of Prestonpans and were parked in Nun's Green. The rest were the so-called "Swedish guns" which had been brought over from France. [39]

Of this number 1,000 men or more may have deserted on the march down. The Jacobites usually took a lenient view of desertion, understanding the foibles of their clansmen and appreciating that they were very much volunteers, and that campaigning a long way from home caused problems with getting in the harvest and looking after their families. Most clansmen who deserted eventually returned to their regiments of their own free will. However, along the way they had managed to recruit the 300 or so men of the Manchester regiment, although they could in no way compare with the hardened warriors of the highland regiments most of whom had been accustomed to bear, and use, arms since their early teens. All in all, the Jacobite army at Derby may have numbered between 5,000 and 6,000 men.

Most of the cavalry were lowland Scots recruited from Aberdeenshire, always a strong Jacobite recruiting ground, and Edinburgh. The Lifeguards, in particular, were well-dressed and equipped wearing blue coats faced with red, red waistcoats and black tricorn hats with a white cockade and a tartan sash worn across the left shoulder. Pitsligo's Horse probably wore some form of highland dress – perhaps a tartan jacket and trews (all the cavalry wore trews or trousers – riding in a kilt is not only difficult but extremely uncomfortable!). The most raffish regiment by far was Bagot's Hussars, commanded at this stage not by Bagot himself but by Captain George Hamilton of Redhouse who was later captured at the skirmish of Clifton during the retreat to Scotland. They were clothed in a close-fitting tartan coat with a plaid cloak and trews and a large fur hat. They appear to have carried, unusually, a single edged backsword rather than the double-edged broadsword more commonly carried by other Scots troops. As well as their swords, all of the cavalry were armed with either a carbine or musketoon and many of them carried a pair of pistols as well.

The backbone of the rebel army, however, was the tough hard-marching infantry, especially the highland clan regiments. The lowland regiments of John Roy Stewart, Gordon of Glenbucket, Lord Ogilvy and the Duke of Perth all wore long-tailed coats of some description, often grey or brown, with knee britches, stockings, sometimes a tartan sash and a blue bonnet with a white cockade; their officers normally wore highland dress. The Manchester Regiment wore blue coats with a tartan sash and, again, a white cockade in their blue bonnets or hats. The highland clan regiments were undoubtedly the most distinctive element in the Prince's army and their appearance must have astonished the citizens of Derby. Most of the rank and file were simple Gaelic-speaking clansmen, having no English at all and the vast majority of them had never left the highlands. They were clad in traditional highland dress, the philamor or great kilt, commonly known as the belted plaid, a large rectangle of particoloured woollen cloth, roughly six yards by two, which was belted at the waist to form the kilt, the rest being draped up the back and over the left shoulder where it was secured by a brooch or pin. With this they wore a shirt, often of saffron dyed linen homespun, and plaid or tartan stockings with home-made brogues of tanned leather, rather like an Indian moccasin. At this time there were no distinctive clan tartans, so each clansman would have worn the tartan of his choice, in a variety of setts and often in a dull brown or green colour. Tartans with a red and black sett were particularly popular with officers. The officers in a highland clan regiment would have worn either the belted plaid or, alternatively, tartan trews and waistcoat.

The clansmen were often heavily armed. The "front rank men," the senior rank and file in the clan hierarchy, would normally have a musket of some type. This would either be the French Model 1717 "Charleroi" musket, of which Charles brought a number with him to Scotland or the standard British army musket, the Long Land Pattern usually referred to as the "Brown Bess" of which large quantities were captured after the Battle of Prestonpans. This was a formidable weapon in trained hands. Weighing about 8 lbs and measuring about 60 inches from butt to tip, this was a muzzle-loading flintlock which fired a .75 calibre soft lead ball weighing about 1.3 ounces. It was reasonably accurate up to about 50 yards, but after that depended on mass volley fire against a large target for its effect. In addition the more senior "front rank" clansmen would have carried a shield or "targe", a highland dirk ("biodag") and the highland weapon par excellence, the broadsword or "claidheamh mor". This formidable weapon, double-edged and about 2.5 feet in length with a basket hilt of brass or iron to protect the hand, could easily lop off an arm or a head at one blow in the hands of an experienced swordsman. At Prestonpans the Chevalier de Johnstone had noted "the field of battle presented a spectacle of horror, being covered with heads, legs, arms and mutilated bodies, for the killed all fell by the sword" and told of one of the highland clansmen, "…about fourteen years of age, scarcely formed, who was presented to the Prince as a prodigy, having killed, as it was said, fourteen of the enemy. The Prince asked him if this was true? 'I do not know' replied he, ' if I killed them; but I brought fourteen soldiers to the ground with my sword.'" In addition to these weapons the officers would have carried one or two pistols and sometimes even more. Before Prestonpans, a Major Stewart, being rather weighed down on the march, was helped by a friend who discovered that he was in possession of two small pistols, two larger pistols with double barrels and a blunderbuss! The common soldiers of the clan regiment, those without the means to purchase expensive items like broadswords, would have carried a musket and bayonet with a dirk and sometimes more traditional clan weapons such as the Lochaber Axe. Altogether the Jacobite army must have presented a savage and alarming prospect to the quiet little country town of Derby which had surely never before seen anything like it. [40]

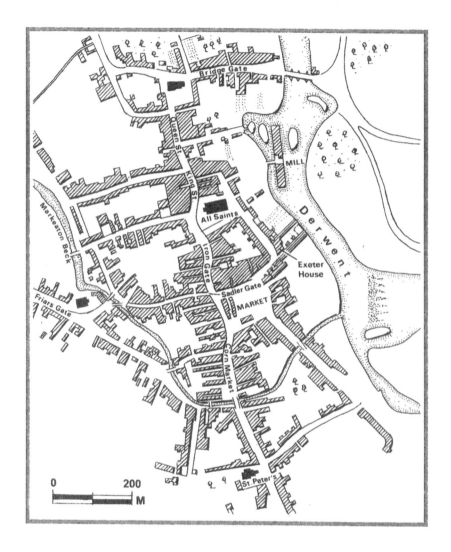

4. Derby in 1745

The first problem for the Jacobites, and for the inhabitants of Derby for that matter, was finding billets for the officers and men. Exeter House was chosen as the quarters for Prince Charles and his immediate entourage. This was situated on the banks of the River Derwent, roughly where the Bonnie Prince Charlie statue is today, with its front facing Full Street and its garden sloping down to the river. The house had been built in 1635 and was in the ownership of Brownlow Cecil, 8th Earl of Exeter, who had inherited it through his wife, the younger daughter of the lead merchant Thomas Chambers. The house was demolished in 1854, but, fortunately, not only was the panelling saved from the room where the Council of War took place next day (and now furnishes the Bonnie Prince Charlie Room at Derby Museum), but we also have an excellent description of the house by a Mrs Katherine Thomson dating from the early 19th century:-

"The house stands back from Full Street and is situated within a small rectangular court...it is devoid of pretension; its gables and chimneys proclaim the Elizabethan period [this was wrong – as mentioned above it was actually built during the Stuart period]. A wide staircase, rising from a small hall, leads to a square oak panelled drawing room, the Presence Chamber in the days of the ill fated Charles. On either side are chambers...retaining much of the character of former days, but garnished recently...The back of Exeter House is picturesque in the extreme. The character of the house is here more distinctly ancient; and its architecture is uniform, though simple. Beyond the steps by which you descend from a spacious drawing room is a long lawn enclosed between high walls and extending to the brink of the River Derwent". [41]

The remaining senior Jacobite commanders were lodged with their staff in the larger town houses, of which Derby boasted a considerable number. The Duke of Atholl was lodged at the house of Alderman Thomas Gisborne which may have been on the Wardwick or, alternatively, at Bridgegate in what is now the Convent of the Sisters of Mercy next to St Mary's church. The Duke of Perth occupied Mr Rivett's house at 14 Tenant Street and Lord Elcho, commander of the cavalry, and one of the more enterprising Jacobite leaders, at 28 Market Place, the home of Thomas Storer. Lord George Murray was billeted at the home of Alderman Heathcote on Full Street, conveniently adjacent to Exeter House (Heathcote may well have been a Jacobite supporter). The raffish and elderly Lord Pitsligo who was aged 67 at the time, found suitable lodgings at the Meynell house on Irongate, now the European Restaurant. Newcastle House on the Market Place was in the ownership of a Mr Kay and had lately been the home of Alderman Joshua Smith and it accommodated the even more elderly septuagenarian John Gordon of Glenbucket. Last, but not least, the Jacobite ladies who had accompanied their husbands on campaign, including Lady Murray and Lady Ogilvy, who was described at the time as "very beautiful," were lodged in the house of Alderman Henry Franceys on the Market Place and which survives, in part, as the Walkabout Pub. Bingham's House (now Lloyds

Bank), on the corner of Irongate and Sadler Gate, was occupied by John Murray, Earl of Nairne who commanded one of the regiments in the Prince's army, and was a cousin of Lord George Murray [42]

The rest of the army had to find lodgings wherever they could. The quartermasters had, of course, sought billets for 9,000 men although, as we have seen, the army at this stage was probably only about 5 to 6,000 strong, but even accommodation for this number must have proved difficult in a town which only had 6,000 inhabitants. The *Gentleman's Magazine* gives the following numbers of soldiers accommodated in each parish for the first and second nights of the occupation:

Parish	First Night	Second Night
St Werburgh's	1990	1641
All Saint's	2979	3007
St Peter's	1091	1002
St Michael's	724	724
St Alkmund's	714	755

However, this was apparently based on an informal survey carried out by local people and supplied to the *Derby Mercury*. It must have been next to impossible to count the numbers accurately, and avoiding double counting would no doubt have been a substantial problem. At all events, as one would expect, we can be sure that the bulk of highland army was lodged in the centre of town in the parishes of All Saints and St Werburgh's. Space was at a premium and the *Gentleman's Magazine* comments that:-

"Many common ordinary houses, both public and private, had 40 or 50 men each, and some gentlemen near 100. At their coming in they were generally treated with bread, cheese, beer and ale, whilst all hands were aloft getting their supper ready; after supper, being weary with their long march, they went to bed, most upon straw, and others in beds." [43]

There are differing accounts of how the Jacobites were received and how they conducted themselves in Derby depending, one suspects, on the political bias of the commentator. A number of letters from Jacobite soldiers to their families in Scotland were captured in

Derby post office after the army retreated, and two of them give a decidedly optimistic impression, this one from Alexander Blair to his wife:-

"The 3rd we came to Ashbourne, and on the 4th arrived here in Derby. At every town we were received with ringing of Bells, and at Night we have Bone fires and Illuminations. I hear Gen. Wade is behind us, and the D[uke] of Cumberland and Gen. Ligonier upon one hand of us, but we are nearer to London than any of them, and it is thought we are designed to march straight there being only ninety miles from it; but tho' both these forces should unite and attack us we do not fear them, for our whole Army is in top spirits, and we trust in God to make a good account of them." [44]

And from Peter Ouchterlony to his wife Jean in Dundee:-

"Wee arrived here last night amidst the acclamations of the people, and publick rejoicings which wee have had in severall places, and we are now within a hundred miles of London without seeing the face of one enemy, so that in a short time I hope to write to you from London, where if we gett safe, the whole of our story and even what has happened already must appear to posterity liker a Romance than anything of truth." [45]

Whig and government supporters, and some of the more fastidious members of the upper classes, took rather a different view of the irruption of the highland army into Derbyshire's county town. One Derby gentleman, in a letter of 13th December and published in the *Daily Post* on 26th December, commented unfavourably on the behaviour of the highlanders billeted on him and even took exception to their piety at mealtimes:-

"[they] looked like so many fiends turned out of hell to ravage the Kingdom and cut throats, and, under their plaids nothing but various sort of butchering weapons were to be seen. But really what did afford me some matter for an unavoidable laughter...was to see these desperadoes, from officers to the common men, at their several meals, first pull off their bonnets, and then lift up their eyes in a most solemn manner, and mutter something to themselves, by way of saying grace, as if they had been so many pure primitive Christians. Their language seems to be as if a herd of Hottentots, wild monkeys in a desert, or

vagrant gypsies had been jabbering screaming and howling together."
[46]

The Derby Mercury gave an equally uncomplimentary impression:-

"Being refreshed with a night's rest, they were very alert the next day, running about from one shop to another, to buy, or rather steal, tradesmen's goods, viz gloves, buckles, powder flasks, buttons, handkerchiefs etc, if they liked a person's shoes better than their own, demanding them off their feet, without pay. The longer they staid the more insolent and outrageous they grew, demanding everything by threats, drawn swords, and pistols clapp'd to the breasts of many persons, not only by the common men but their officers; so that several persons were obliged to abscond to preserve their lives." [47]

The family of Mrs Sarah Wightman (born in 1767) had a house in Green Lane, and as a small child her grandmother told her about the Jacobite occupation of the town and how it had affected their family; she in turn related those events to her grandson, Alfred Wallis, some time editor of the Derby Mercury who recorded her recollections in notes attached to the Order of Service for the thanksgiving service held on 9th October 1746. They are now in the possession of the Derby Local Studies Library:-

"They ran beer into top boots and drank from it, cut cheeses into half and held the cut side over the fire and scraped off the cheese as it melted, scattered straw over the floors of the best rooms and slept in it …like pigs and smoked tobacco to the great danger of setting fire to the straw. They took all the arms they could lay hands on, even to an old cross bow that hung in the garret, and helped themselves freely to clothes and books. There was a piper amongst them who, when not engaged in eating and drinking, was continually piping. When they departed they warned the household to keep indoors as they would soon return, and, if not obeyed, would cut all their throats when they came back. The house was filled with vermin and was not fit for habitation for some time after they left. The officers mostly spoke in French and kept their men in pretty good order".[48]

Another long-lived Derby woman, Mrs Katherine Thomson (see above for her description of Exeter House), had an account of life in

Derby during the occupation from her grandmother who had been present as a young woman and recalled the enthusiasm that there was in some quarters for the Jacobite cause:-

"The ladies of Derby vied with each other in making white cockades, of delicate and costly workmanship, to present to the hero of the day. To some of these admiring votaries he presented his picture, a dangerous gift in aftertimes, when a strict system of scrutiny prevailed; and when even to be suspected of Jacobite principles was an effectual barrier to promotion in offices, and a severe injury to those in trade. One of these Jacobite ladies is known by her family to have kept the portrait of the Prince behind the door of her bedchamber, carefully veiled from any but friendly inspection." [This was Mrs Thomson's grandmother]. [49]

It is certainly true that many of the female inhabitants of Derby, as in other towns that the Prince had marched through on his journey south, were captivated by the romance of the occasion and by the Prince's personal charm and charisma, and we do know that he presented gifts to some of the ladies of the town. While his quarters were at Exeter House, he took his meals at the home of a Mrs Ward, who was the widow of a long-serving Alderman of the town. Her 13 year old son, Samuel, tasted the Prince's food before each meal and before he left the Prince presented a gold and diamond ring to his mother which is now in the possession of Derby Museum.

While the Prince dined out at Mrs Ward's, his entourage also purchased food and drink for use at Exeter House. We know exactly what was bought from the entries in the Prince's Household Book (his record of domestic expenses which was scrupulously kept for most of the campaign):-

paid for bread	0.17.0
paid for alle [ale]	0.13.4
for Limons, Eggs, Floure, and Root, for veal	0. 3. 0.
for pertridges, foul & fish	0.15.0
to 8 pd butter at 6d	0. 4 .0
to eggs	0. 1. 2
to 4 bottles Beere	0. 1. 0. [50]

Once billeting arrangements had been made, the quartermasters set about levying a contribution from the town. This was something they had done in every town of any size through which the army had passed on its way south and in Lancashire alone they had raised some £1,200. In Derby itself a total of about £500 was raised by subscription from Jacobite "supporters", apparently without significant difficulty, although it is clear that many people were not willing contributors but paid up for fear of the consequences if they did not. Mr Heathcote, at whose house was lodged Lord George Murray, provided, under duress, a list of all those in the town who had subscribed to the expenses of raising a regiment, the Derbyshire Blues, of whom more in Chapter 7. They were then required to pay a similar sum towards the expenses of the Prince's army (see Appendix 8). The Hanoverian spy Thomas Drake, who was then in Derby under cover, reported that the town crier was sent to order payment of any outstanding excise duty by 5 p.m. that day, no doubt causing consternation to Derby's considerable number of ale houses and brewers. The sum of £100 was demanded at the Post Office and also payment of six month's land tax. According to the Derby historian Glover, the total amount raised was about £3,000, but a more accurate calculation gives a figure of £500 raised by "voluntary" subscription and a further £665.12.8 from seizure of "public monies" from the Post Office. This was probably customs, excise and other government taxes which had been collected, rather than cash belonging to the municipality. At the Virgin's Inn, on the corner of the Market Place and Full Street, hay and corn to a value of £1.16.00 was levied for the use of the Prince's cavalry. [51]

Not surprisingly, the inhabitants of Derby were much concerned with the possibility of looting by the highland army, and many of the leading citizens had left the town taking their more valuable possessions with them. John Daniel, the ensign in Balmerino's troop of the Prince's Lifeguard gave a lively account of this on first entering the town:-

"Derby is a large and handsome town. The heads of it were much terrified at our entrance, many of them having made large subscriptions to Government [this is a reference to the subscriptions taken up for the Derbyshire Blues a few days before] and therefore had quitted their houses with the utmost precipitation. It fell to my lot to be quartered in one of them, viz one Mr Chambers. Coming in with my billet, I asked if I could lodge there. The Steward immediately replied that I could adding 'and anything we can do for you, shall be done: only pity us in our situation, which is most deplorable.' At this wondering much what he meant, I told him to be of good courage that neither I nor any of us were come to hurt him or anyone. Having thus abated the horrid notion they had of us.......he conducted me to the Housekeeper, who was also in tears. She was somewhat seized with horror at the sight, though my countenance was none of the roughest: but soon collected herself and made the same answer with the utmost feminine tenderness, putting themselves and the whole house under my mercy. I truly was much surprised, for anything of this kind was quite new to me: however, after pulling off my riding-coat and boots she conducted me into a fine room where, at entering, I perceived a number of jewels and watches lying confusedly up and down........I demanded to whom they belonged, and what was the reason of their being so carelessly laid up.......'Sir' said she 'Mr Chambers, the master of this house, no enemy to you, has retired with his lady and family to the country'. 'Why so?' said I. 'Not conscious' replied she 'of anything particular against you, but out of fear of what the Highlanders might do against him.' She then begged that I would have compassion on them, and be their protector, which, after some short discourse, I promised.......I then ordered all the things that lay so confusedly thrown about, to be locked up, assuring them, that nothing should be touched or broke open, unless with authority. So for two days I ruled master there, and, I hope they will generously acknowledge, much to their content and satisfaction in that situation of affairs having preserved the Young Lady's jewels from the hand of rapine, and hindered the house from being damaged." [52]

While these important financial matters were being attended to in Derby, clothes, shoes, arms, horses and fodder were being seized both in the town itself and in the outlying villages and towns. As soon as the Jacobites had occupied Derby, a strong force of eighty men was sent to seize the bridge over the River Trent at Swarkestone; this was of great strategic importance because it commanded the lowest crossing point of the river and carried the London road. In the meantime advanced parties of the highland army had got as far as Smalley, Wirksworth, and, it is said, Loughborough, a strongly Tory and Jacobite town where two quartermasters appeared in order to requisition billets for the army. Dudley Bradstreet (see Chapter 8), whose evidence needs to be treated with considerable caution, says that he encountered three Jacobite soldiers at an alehouse on the Burton side of Derby (perhaps the Egginton Arms) and a local tradition at Smalley has it that a party of highlanders visited Smalley Hall and there seized horses belonging to a

Mrs Richardson. A well-attested incident occurred at Kedleston Hall where the owner, Sir Nathaniel Curzon, supposedly a Tory supporter, was in residence but keeping a very low profile. A requisitioning party of Jacobite horse called to see him late in the evening of 5th December. Dr Mather, Curzon's chaplain, recorded their arrival in a letter to Sir Nathaniel's son:-

"On Thursday night (i.e. 5th December), between 11 and 12, as I was going to bed, I heard a great rapping at the gate. "Who's there?" "King James's men" they answered. Down went I, and by that time they were got to the east gates. They said they must come in. I told them it was a late hour to make a visit. One (that I afterwards found was an officer) spoke more civilly than the rest, and said that he must come in and speak with Sir Nathaniel. I told him he was abed. He said he must see him. I told him what commands he had to Sir Nathaniel, I would carry. And so bid the servants to open the gates, and show'd them into the servants' hall. There were about six or seven highlanders armed hussar fashion [these were Bagot's Hussars], each with a brace of pistols in their hands, and a brace in their girdles, a broad sword, and one or two of them had a musket slung on his shoulder. That rascal Hewit, brother to the man that mends the roads, was with them, and I believe was the man that brought them thither. He has listed with them at Derby." [53]

Amidst all this frenetic activity, the Prince did not lose sight of the necessity to give thanks to God for the safe arrival of his army at Derby, and on the morning of Thursday 5th December all the officers and men were ordered to attend a service at All Saints Church. The circumstances of this service have given rise to considerable controversy since it was suggested, in Cox's "Chronicles of the Collegiate Church of All Saints" published in 1881, that the service in question was, in fact, a Roman Catholic Mass [54]. There is little or no evidence to support this apart from Cox's bare assertion of the fact and, indeed, all the evidence tends to point the other way. To Roman Catholics the church, being a Protestant one, would not have been considered properly consecrated for the purpose of celebrating Mass and, in any event, so far was we know there was no Roman Catholic chaplain with the Jacobite army. There was, however, an Anglican cleric, Thomas Coppock, who was chaplain to the Manchester Regiment, and it is probable that it was he who conducted the service which would have been a normal Church of England eucharist. None of the Jacobite officers present who left an account of the occupation of Derby mentions a Catholic Mass being celebrated, and in his journal the highland officer John McLean (paymaster of McLean's regiment) simply notes:-

"Thursday the 5th/Decembr we rested and in the evening we were ordered to goe hear prayers in the handsome church of All Saints where there is a very fine new Organs [sic]." [55]

It is interesting to note that there is a discrepancy about the time of the service in this account, and it is quite possible that more than one service was held, perhaps Eucharist in the morning and Evensong in the evening. With some 6,000 Jacobite soldiers in Derby, including several hundred officers, it would not have been possible to fit them all into the church for one service, and one suspects that it was, in fact, only the officers who attended.

Furthermore, the Prince wore his Catholicism lightly at this time in order not to deter non-Catholic Jacobites from supporting him, and it is clear from his comments at the time that he would have been perfectly prepared to forego the religion of his father and grandfather if, by doing so, he could have established himself with his British subjects. It is almost unthinkable that he would have acted so provocatively and insensitively as to have had Mass said in a Protestant Church in a town that was almost exclusively either Church of England or dissenting Protestant and at a time when he desperately needed to attract adherents to his army; they would undoubtedly have been deterred if they thought that by doing so they were helping to re-establish Catholicism in England. We now know that the Prince, in 1750, returned secretly to England, abjured his Catholic faith and became a member of the established church. All in all, therefore, we can dispose of Cox's suggestion that Mass was said at All Saints as improbable in the extreme.

All this activity on the part of the invaders still left time for some leisure, and amid all the drama there were some amusing incidents to lighten the mood. In the evening the Duke of Perth asked for a newspaper and the *St James's Evening-Post* was brought to him. It contained the following satirical article about Jacobites, the supposed birth of King James III (the warming pan allegation referred to above in Chapter 1), and their alleged support by the Catholic Church, masquerading under the guise of an advertisement for some missing dogs:-

"Run away from their Master at Rome, in the Dog-Days of last August and since secreted in France, two young Lurchers, of the right Italian Breed; and being of a black Tan Colour, with sharp Noses, long Claws, and hanging Ears, have been taken Abroad for King Charles the Second's Breed; but a Bitch from Italy unfortunately broke the Strain in 88, by admitting into the Kennel, a base Mongrel of another Litter - They are supposed to be on the Hunt for Prey in the North. they go a full Dog-Trot by night for fear of being catch'd. They answer to the names of Hector and Plunder, and will jump and dance at the Sound of the French Horn, being used to that Note by an old Dog-Master at Paris. they prick up their Ears also at the Musick of a Lancashire Hornpipe.

This is to give Notice that whoever can secure this Couple of curs, and bring them back, either to the Pope's Head at Rome, near St Peter's Church, or to the Cardinal's Cap at Versailles, or to the King's Arms at Newcastle, or to the Thistle at Edingburg, or to the Three King's at Brentford or rather to the Sign of the Axe on Tower-Hill, shall have the Reward of Thirteen-pence Half-penny or any sum below a Crown, and the Thanks of all the Powers of Europe except France, Spain and the Pope.

N.B. They have each a French Collar on, stamp'd with their Father's Arms, a Warming Pan, and the Flower de Lis with this inscription; We are but Young Puppies of Tencin's-Pack.

Beware of them for they have got a Smack of the Scots-Mange and those that are bit by them run mad and are called JACO-BITES." [56]

No doubt in the mood of euphoria induced by the entry into Derby, the Duke and his followers could afford to laugh at the joke. Whether they still felt like laughing two days later must be a moot point.

There were other light-hearted incidents as well. The Mayor of Derby, Robert Hague, who had made himself conveniently absent at the Jacobites' entry into the town, returned the next day and decided (no doubt hedging his bets) that he should attend Exeter House and present himself to the Prince. He duly announced himself as the Mayor but, forgetting himself for a moment, foolishly told the sentries that he was seeking an audience with "the Pretender". For this rather unfortunate lapse in memory he was kicked down the stairs by the highland guard with the words "Rascal that you are, if you want to see a Pretender, you should go to St James's!" [57]

So far as recruits were concerned, Derby was a bitter disappointment. James Sparkes, mentioned above as offering himself and five hundred stout fellows as recruits, predictably did not fulfil his promise. In fact only five men, so far as we are aware, joined the Prince's army from Derby or Derbyshire: James Sparkes, the framework knitter, Charles Webster and William Morris, occupations unknown, Edward Hewit, mentioned in Mather's letter quoted above, who was a butcher, and Humphrey Cook, a blacksmith. The fate of these unfortunate men will be covered in Chapter 11.

Having failed to raise any substantial support for his endeavours in Derby, therefore, it now fell to the Prince and his advisers, the senior Jacobite commanders who marched with the army into England, to decide what next to do, for which purpose a council of war was convened at Exeter House. This was a tangled affair which deserves a chapter of its own.

Chapter 7

The Hanoverian Government's Response

While all these dramatic events were taking place in Derby, what was the government up to? It had, of course, been doing its best to react to a rapidly changing and often unpredictable series of events ever since the Prince had landed in Scotland in July.

As soon as the initial success of the rising became clear, and especially after the stunning and wholly unexpected victory of the Prince's army at Prestonpans (Gladsmuir to the Jacobites), the government began to recall its troops from Flanders, together with Dutch troops and some Swiss troops in Dutch pay who were allied to the British under the terms of the Treaty of Utrecht which had brought an end to the War of the Spanish Succession in 1713. The Dutch troops were the first to arrive on 19th and 20th September. Most remained in and around London, but some were sent to Newcastle to reinforce Field Marshal Wade. The first withdrawals of regular British troops arrived in the Thames on 23rd September, and all the remaining troops, together with their commander William Augustus Duke of Cumberland, the King's third son, arrived in mid-October, by which time the Prince's army was already recuperating after Prestonpans and was soon to embark on its fateful decision to invade England.

By the time the Jacobite army commenced its invasion on 8th November, the government forces deployed to oppose it were as follows:-

Wade's forces in Newcastle totalling some 12,600 men including 4,200 Dutch and Swiss infantry. These latter were notoriously bloody-minded and intractable, and being essentially mercenaries had little interest in the outcome of the rising except insofar as it affected their pay.

Lt General Roger Handasyde's forces at Berwick-upon-Tweed. These were the remnants of Cope's forces that had escaped south after the Battle of Prestonpans and were available either to reinforce Wade at Newcastle or to march north and reinforce the remaining government troops in Scotland. They numbered about 1,500 men consisting of 2 regiments of Dragoons and 2 battalions of infantry. They re-occupied Edinburgh in early November.

Lt General Sir John Ligonier's forces in the Midlands, numbering about 10,500 men. These were concentrated in the West

Midlands around Stone, Stafford and Lichfield and thus were the nearest government troops to Derby at the time of the occupation. Lord George Murray had given them the slip by feinting towards Wales and then doubling back through Leek as described above. From 23rd November the elderly Ligonier was replaced and the Midland forces fell under the direct command of the Duke of Cumberland who was also the supreme commander of all the government forces in Britain. In addition to the above, there was also a small force of Dragoons in Chester numbering about 2,000 men.

By the time the Jacobite army reached Derby, a further force composed partly of raw recruits, was being formed on Finchley Common to protect London; these were the subject of Hogarth's famous etching "The March to Finchley." However, there were also four battalions of experienced infantry from Flanders, Mordaunts's, Huske's, Bragg's and Beauclerks's, and a large train of artillery was being made ready at the Tower of London in preparation for a march to Finchley when required. This consisted of some 34 pieces of artillery with 240 trained gunners to man them, a much more formidable force of guns than the Jacobites ever managed to muster. [58]

As the Jacobite army marched steadily into England, Wade's army shadowed them from across the Pennines. Wade himself was 72 at the time and well past his prime as an active campaigner. His attempts to deflect the Jacobites were tardy and ineffective. We have already seen how he attempted a march across the Pennines through deep snow on 17th November which ended in a fiasco on 19th November when his utterly weary and frozen troops heard that Carlisle had fallen and retreated back to Newcastle having achieved nothing. In fairness to Wade, however, it is right to say that the winter of 1745 was once of the coldest and most severe for many years. Thereafter Wade marched his army south keeping a parallel course with the Prince but showing no great signs of urgency. By 6th December, when the Jacobites had decided to leave Derby, he had only reached Doncaster and was a good two day's march from the Prince with no chance whatever of cutting him off from the London road, and he had lost some 700 men along the way - the Jacobite army could, of course, outmarch the average British soldier by a substantial margin.

The government's main hope of opposing the Highland army lay in the Midlands army now commanded by Cumberland who, whatever his faults, was a dedicated professional soldier with two campaigns under his belt. By 29th November, while the Jacobite army was entering Manchester, the Duke had the following forces at his disposal, some of which had been newly raised and were thus untried in battle:-

Cavalry

Ligonier's Regiment	- Stone
Kingston's Regiment	- Cheadle and Uttoxeter (one squadron at each) - newly raised
Bland's Regiment	- Newcastle-under-Lyme
Lord Mark Kerr's	- Trentham, Stoke & Darlaston
Cobham's	- Northampton
Montagu's	- Marching to Burton on Trent - newly raised

Infantry

Bligh's	- Chester
Cholmondleys	- Chester - newly raised
Gower's	- Chester - newly raised
Herbert's	- Frodsham - newly raised
Soule's	- Stafford
Johnson's	- Stafford
Semphill's	- Stafford
Douglas's	- Stafford
North British Fusiliers	- Stafford
Skelton's	- Lichfield
Bedford's	- Lichfield - newly raised
Howard's	- Tamworth
Handasyde's	- Coventry or Coleshill
Granby's	- Warwick - newly raised
Halifax's	- Shrewsbury - newly raised
Ordnance foot	- Warwick
Guards	- Barkwell & Dunchurch
Artillery	- Lichfield

By the time the Jacobites had entered Derby, the forces gathering at Finchley to protect the capital consisted of the following:-

Cavalry

Horse guards
Horse Grenadiers
Ligonier's 8th Horse
1st Royal Dragoons (Hawley's)
4th Dragoons (Rich)

Infantry
Foot Guards
1st Royal Scots (St Clair's)
Mordaunt's
Huske's
Bragg's
Beauclerk's
Richbell's
Murray's (the Black Watch)

Artillery
The forces mentioned at page 79 above which were being prepared at the Tower of London [59]

In total the forces awaiting Prince Charles at Finchley numbered some 6,000 men with more on the way, excluding the powerful train of artillery which the Jacobites could not possibly match. The government forces in the Midlands in and around Stafford and Lichfield, or on their way there, could not have numbered less than 11,000 men - thus the government forces outnumbered the Jacobite army by at least three to one. This was an infinitely more powerful force than the government had been able to field hitherto and, moreover, it was composed very largely of experienced Flanders troops, veterans of the hard fight with the French at Fontenoy and elsewhere.

So much for the government's regular forces. What of the local forces with which they hoped to oppose the invaders? As well as the regular army, there was a long-established system of part-time soldiers, the Militia, which was supposed to be available for home defence. These were volunteers who received some slight training annually and worked at their normal occupations for the rest of the year. Few of them had any previous military experience - they were essentially the butcher the baker and the candlestick maker who joined up for the sake of the uniform, an annual camp, often simply a glorified drinking session, and the spurious sense of superiority which enabled them to shine amongst their peers. Their officers were usually drawn from the gentry or merchant class, and few of them had any experience of active campaigning.

In each county it was the responsibility of the Lord Lieutenant to embody, train and arm the militia in time of need. As the Jacobites advanced steadily into England, the county militias were mustered up and down the northern counties, but this was more for show than anything else - none of them came into action against the Scots and, had they done so, they would almost certainly have been cut to pieces by the tough, experienced and by now well-armed highlanders; prudently, they kept out of the way. In addition, many independent "association troops" were raised, paid for by subscription. Such troops were raised in Yorkshire, Lancashire, Cheshire and other northern counties. In Lancashire the "Lancashire Blues" proved to be such a liability that they were disbanded after only 12 days when their pay ran out.

In Derbyshire the incumbent Lord Lieutenant was William, 3rd Duke of Devonshire, scion of one of the most important Whig families in the country, the Cavendishes, and based at the family home at Chatsworth [60]. He was the grandson of the 1st Duke who had engineered the deposition of James II from his throne in 1688, and was one of the conspirators that hatched the plot at Revolution House in Old Whittington near Chesterfield. The Duke had acceded to the title on the death of his father in 1729 and had just returned from Ireland after six years as Lord Lieutenant. In 1718 he had married for love, unusually for a Cavendish, Katherine Hoskyns, the daughter of a city financier and was devoted to his wife and children. He was described by a contemporary as "Plain in his manners and negligent in his dress" and by the arch Tory Dr Samuel Johnson as "not a man of superior abilities, but a man faithful to his word". He seems to have been somewhat tardy in responding to the emergency. Lord Charles Cavendish, had recently written a letter to his nephew, the Marquis of Hartington, which indicates that the Duke was rather more concerned about protecting his property than anything else:-

"You say nothing about packing up your medals. If the French should land there would probably be a rising here. In which case, I very much doubt that there would be time to carry things away." [61]

On 28th September the Duke convened a meeting of the gentry and justices of the county at the George Inn on Irongate, Derby (now the Mr Jorrocks Pub). In his diary entry for 27th September James Clegg, recorded:-

"All about in a great consternation under apprehensions of the progress of the Rebellion, our Gentlemen set out to meet the Duke of Devonshire at Derby to concert measures for raising forces for the defence of the nation." [62]

The meeting was well-attended, and it was decided that a regiment of 500 men (or, alternatively, two smaller regiments of 250 men each) would be raised, fifty men in each of ten companies to be distributed as follows:-

Derby	- 2 Companies
Ashbourne	- 1 Company
Chesterfield	- 2 Companies
Alfreton	- 1 Company
Bakewell & Tideswell	- 1 Company
Sudbury & Hilton	- 1 Company
Duffield & Belper	- 1 Company
Repton	- 1 Company

The officers of the two Derby companies were listed in the minutes of the meeting:-

CAPTAINS

John Gisborne Jnr (presumably a son of Thomas Gisborne who owned the Jacobean House on the Wardwick and had been a Mayor of Derby)

William Roberts

Thomas Rivett

Gilbert Cheshire

LIEUTENANTS

Nicholas Thornhill

Frances Rivett (a brother of Thomas)

Mr Blith

ENSIGNS

George Parkhill Jnr

Godfrey Heathcote Jnr (a son of alderman Heathcote who had also been a Mayor of Derby and was a prominent local figure)

SERGEANTS

Mr Mills

Henry Hind

Benjamin Elliott Jnr [63]

Clearly money would be needed to support this new "association regiment" and at the meeting a subscription was taken which realised £6,169, a very considerable sum at the time which, in itself, demonstrates, if not the loyalty of the subscribers, then at least their wish to be seen as supporters of the Hanoverian regime and, perhaps, their anxiety that the present government, and the country, should not be destabilised by this extraordinary attempt to restore the Stuart dynasty to the throne. The wording of the subscription itself makes interesting reading:-

"Whereas a most wicked and unnatural Rebellion is begun in that part of Great Britain called Scotland, by the eldest son of the Pretender, against our rightful sovereign King George, in order to subvert our Religion and Liberties, and to entail popery and Slavery on us and our posterity: We His Majesty's most Loyal Subjects, whose names are hereunto subscribed, do hereby declare our utmost abhorrence of so wicked an attempt; and in the most solemn manner engage, that we will, at the hazard of our Lives and Fortunes, Support and defend our excellent Constitution in Church and State, and oppose all attempts against His Majesty's Person and Government, particularly the Rebellion now carried on in favour of a Popish abjured Pretender. And we hereby promise and engage to meet together from time to time to concert and execute such measures as may be necessary for affecting the purposes of this our Association." [64]

The signatories included members of virtually all of the most prominent families in the county; Meynell; Fitzherbert (a long established Catholic and Royalist family); Okeover; Pole (of which more anon); Harpur (likewise); Vernon; Wilmot; Curzon; and, of course, the Duke himself. A full list of the subscribers may be found at Appendix 7. Significantly, the subscribers included most of the more influential Tory supporters in the county.

There were two subsequent meetings - at the King's Head on Irongate, Derby, on 3rd October when Sir Nathaniel Curzon, and the Marquis of Hartington (eldest son of the Duke of Devonshire), the two MP's for the time being of the County of Derby, were appointed as Colonels of the Regiment, and again on 28th October at the Talbot Inn, Derby, where the pay of the regiment was determined. The captains were to be paid 8/- [40p] per day, corporals 1/6, [8p] drummers 1/3 [7p], and privates 1/- [5p]. Bounty money of 5/- [25p] for each person enlisting would also be paid and £20 to each company of 58 officers and men towards the cost of drums and standards. The uniform was to be a dark blue serge coat with white breeches, black buckled shoes and a black tricorn hat with an orange cockade (orange was the colour of the

Hanoverian supporter as white was for the Jacobite).There was a proviso that enlistment would be for 100 days and that no man could be asked to march more than 10 miles outside the county boundaries. The total cost of raising the regiment was calculated at £1,214.19.6d [£1,214.95p]. Payments to officers included a sum of £52 to Capt Johnson, £11 to the Sergeants, £10 to the Corporals and £4.12.6d [£4.62p] to the drummers. This was presumably "head money." [65]

At the second meeting at the King's Head an important decision was taken not to muster the existing county militia who were considered to be politically unreliable. The local Whigs had convened the first meeting themselves, but some Tory supporters turned up at the second meeting and objected to the taking up of a subscription.

In the meantime arms had been ordered from London to equip the new regiment. On 26th October the Marquis of Hartington wrote to his father:-

"The arms will set out from the Tower on Monday morning, the Steward has been so ill of the Govnt [sic] that it was impossible for him to take any care about them: I was forced to trouble Sir Robt Willmot.......there has been some difficulty about his indenting for them.....I should be much obliged to you if you would send the Black Mare to Derby, because you may depend upon it that I will at all events set out upon the first news....I have directed the arms to Mr Gisborne at Derby. I wish the Drums etc may be ready to be sent down with them". [66]

Three days later the Marquis wrote again to his father:-

"The arms were loaded on two Wagons at the Tower yesterday, but I believe did not leave London till this morning (Saturday) and will be at Derby on Monday next. There are 28 chests containing 700 Musquets, 700 bayonets, 300 and 90 Cartouche Boxes and 900 and 50 Frogs which are the things to carry the Bayonets in, the remaining number of the two last Articles will be sent down as soon as they can be made, for they have no more ready at the Tower". [67]

Further measures were also taken to ensure that potential Jacobite supporters were neutralised. There was the usual panic about the role of Catholics, still regarded in government quarters as a potential fifth column. On 25th September one John Griffin wrote to the Duke that he was apprehensive about "ye Roman Catholics; and our disaffected neighbours even more so than from the Rebells at present" and he opined that if there should be an invasion (of England) "Your Grace may depend upon it they will then Rise, for different parts, and that they have a Watch-word for the purpose". In a letter forwarded to the Duke shortly afterwards by Lord Malton, the Lord Lieutenant of the West Riding of Yorkshire and a most zealous and effective Whig, the informant stated " There are 2 persons in the Parish of Hathersage that are able to depose if compelled to it, their sight of a great number of arms concealed in 2 private rooms at the Duke of Norfolk's, whose names are Robert Ashton and Ann Ashton. They saw the same at Worksop Manner [Manor]. Be cautious in the search; For the within mentioned Rooms have no passage into them, but from the Top of the leads [roof]; the taking up of some part of which will discover the passage into them". Needless to say, no arms were discovered, although a number of prominent Catholics were arrested and the rest told to confine themselves to their estates. [68]

More practical efforts were made to delay the advance of the Highland army by obstructing the roads and removing food, forage and livestock. At a meeting at Ashbourne on 25th November the Deputy Lords Lieutenant and Justices of the Peace resolved to cut the roads at Buxton and elsewhere, and on 30th November the Duke's Steward, Alexander Barker, wrote to the Duke:-

"If there should be any trees by the Road does yr Grace please to have them thrown across it, or if any Hollows should they be filled in: I shall give directions only for three Cutts without I hear from your Grace.....if there be time a cut or two might be made over the Turnpike between Whaley and Chapell but shall not do that without yr Grace's further directions." [69]

It is far from clear how effective these measures were. On 30th November James Clegg wrote in his diary:-

"At home til afternoon, then walked up to Town and spent some time with Mr Duckenfield, sent two men to assist in making trenches to obstruct the Roads about Waley but in my thought it could not answer any good purpose but was very bad for travellers." [70]

By 3rd December, with the more prosperous citizens leaving Derby with their goods and chattels, including Equity Wright, father of the famous painter Joseph Wright of Derby, then aged about 12, the Derbyshire Blues held a review in the Market Place in the afternoon. Realizing the hopelessness of their position, by 10 pm they were marching towards Nottingham, with the Duke at their head, away from the advancing Jacobite army, arriving there in the early hours of the 4th December. There it was decided that the store of gunpowder in the County Magazine at Nottingham Castle should be handed over to the regiment rather than being left at the risk of capture by the rebels if and when they reached the town. The muskets and other weapons in the magazine were also removed and hidden, and the regiment then marched on to Mansfield. From Mansfield, still feeling themselves unsafe, they retreated further to Retford, only a short march from Field Marshal Wade's advancing troops who were at Doncaster. It had been a most inglorious episode, although the outcome would undoubtedly have been much worse if they had stayed in Derby to meet the Prince's army. The movements of the Derbyshire Blues were summarised in a letter from Lord Hartington to his friend Dr Newcombe dated 14th December:-

"... when the Rebels came to Ashbourne, which is ten miles from Derby, as it was impossible for us to think of resisting their whole force, we retired to Nottingham, we had some consultation there about maintaining a Pass over a small Brook between that Town and Derby [probably the River Leen], but after examination it did not prove tenable, so we marched the next day to Mansfield, where we had a false alarm that made us move our Quarters again. We had had flying reports most part of the Day that the Rebels were advancing our Way, which we had given no credit to, but on the contrary had sent a Captain with one Company to take Quarters in the Road towards Derby, in order to return there as soon as ye Highlanders had left it, imagining that they would have gone directly for London; just as it was growing dark our captain returned and assur'd us that he had seen the Rebels to ye number of three or four thousand within two miles of the Town, and this being also confirmed by other advices, we thought it was prudent to get out of their way and we went to Retford....." [71]

The Derbyshire Blues and their commanders have been much criticised for their hasty and ignominious retreat - indeed, it was the subject of a scabrous satirical broadsheet entitled "The Chronicle of the Derbyshire Regiment" (see Appendix 3), no doubt the work of an anonymous Jacobite supporter writing under the pseudonym of "Nathan Ben Shaddai, a priest of the Jews". In truth, however, they had little alternative. None of the other regiments of militia or association troops that had been raised in Westmorland, Cumberland and Lancashire had fared any better. Indeed, rather than face the experienced and battle-hardened highlanders the Lancashire Blues had been disbanded. There can be little doubt that if the Derbyshire Blues had remained in Derby to defend the town against the Prince's army, they would have been slaughtered to a man. The defence of the county, and of the country as a whole, would have to depend in the last analysis on the regular army, the veterans of the campaign in Flanders who had been hastily brought home to meet the threat.

Chapter 8

Spies, Charlatans and Informers

Whilst the government's regular forces might have been wrong-footed by the Jacobite invasion, and their association troops ill-trained and inadequate to meet the threat, their intelligence service appears to have been well-developed and widespread. In and around Derby there were several spies, official and unofficial, active in providing the authorities with details of the Jacobite advance and of their numbers and composition. In Derby itself there were two spies who reported on the entry of the highland army into the town on the morning of Wednesday 4th December, Thomas Drake and Henry Bracken. Bracken wrote:-

"the common soldiers are a most despicable crew, being in general less in stature, and of a wan and meagre countenance, stepping along under their arms with difficulty." [72]

Thomas Drake, who seems to have been active throughout the whole of the occupation, described the appearance of the Jacobite army in more detail:-

"the officers and indeed the Horse in general are likely men, but the foot are sure the poorest scoundrels that ever was seen. They are in generall very indifferently armed; few or none but the officers were what we call completely armed. Their pistols are indifferent, but their firelocks are very bad."[73]

Another correspondent to the government, George English, described the Scots in even more denigrating terms, and eccentric spelling:-

"In short the Hole of the men and Cannon near the Poorest That Ever was seen To pass through a Countrey, men Women and children Did not Amount to 8,000 to the utmost and scarce 2,000 fit to face a good Army, poorly armed for Genneral part; Sum shoes sum nighther shoe or stocken. I durst be Bold to Venture To say That 3 Rigiments of Dragoos and Two of foot would cut them all to pieces." [74]

Whilst these accounts accord with the information sent by Derby residents to the *Gentleman's Magazine*, and published there (see Chapter 6 above and Appendix 5), and whilst they might very well have been an accurate picture of the rank and file of the Jacobite army, appearances could be very deceptive as the Battle of Prestonpans had demonstrated; a ragged and half armed highland clansman had proved himself, man for man, to be a superior soldier to a government regular. One also doubts the observation that the rebels "firelocks are very bad." Substantial quantities of excellent ordnance issue British muskets, the famous "Brown Bess," had been captured at Prestonpans and many of the clansmen were armed with them. In any event, the highlanders were much less dependent on their firearms than a conventional army, relying as they did on the highland charge and the use of their broadswords.

Apart from these amateur spies, it is clear that the government also had in place some much more professional agents. During his advance through Staffordshire Lord George Murray heard of the precipitate departure from Congleton of the Duke of Kingston; having billeted his troops there and enjoyed the Duke's dinner, still left warm on the table, he decided to send a patrol of horse to Newcastle-under-Lyme under William Boyd, Earl of Kilmarnock, commander of Kilmarnock's Horse and accompanied by the Jacobite army's Scoutmaster General, Colonel Henry Kerr of Graden. At the little village of Talke they surprised a party of dragoons at the Red Lion Inn; with them was Cumberland's most important spy, Roger Vere (sometimes spelt Weir). Most of the Dragoons managed to escape but Vere was captured, a great loss to the Hanoverian intelligence system because he had been shadowing the Jacobites for many days and had sent back much accurate and useful information about their numbers and direction of march. He was still a captive with the rebel army on 13th December as it retreated north through Lancaster but was ultimately rescued when Cumberland re-captured Carlisle at the end of the month.

Another government spy who had the misfortune to be captured was the linen draper Eleizer Birch. He had left London for Manchester at 6 pm on Monday 2nd December leaving there on the following day and arriving in Derby in the early evening of Tuesday 3rd December. After a complicated series of journeys, which involved visits to Findern, Uttoxeter and, finally, Stafford, where he gave information to Cumberland, he returned again to Derby thinking that by then the Jacobites would have left. Arriving back in Derby again on the evening of Thursday 5th December he was questioned by the sentries, who being suspicious, arrested him. He was taken, with his guide, to Exeter House (the Prince's headquarters) where both were interrogated. His guide seems to have broken down and admitted that they had both been to the Duke's headquarters at Stafford, and Birch was then taken before John Hay of Restalrig, a senior Jacobite officer and later Secretary of State to the Prince, for more detailed questioning. He was threatened with hanging and then imprisoned in an attic room from which he made a dramatic escape. Let him tell his story in his own words:-

" ....at last I was left alone and then I began to think of making my escape, and the first thing that I did in order to it was to try whether I cou'd open the sashes, one I found was nailed, the other I open'd the shutter of and raised the lower sash a little but was interupted by a person coming into the room who proving none of my guard seem'd to take little notice of me and went out again, upon which I boulted the door on the inside and made shift to get of my boots and imediately after flung myself out of the window under which was a hard gravel walk in Lord Exeter's garden. The height of the window from the walk was, as has since been computed, above 7 yards. I was pretty much stun'd with the fall but soon recover'd myself and ran down the garden wch at the bottom is bounded by the river Darwent and inclosed by high brick walls on each side at the end of which to the water long iron spikes were drove to prevent, as I apprehend, the comunication betwixt that and the adjoyning gardens.......I afterwards ran across two more gardens.....until I came to Mr Heathcote's, which I found to be a high brick wall, upon laying hold of it at the lower end part of the wall fell and forced me into the river which in that place is several yards deep. It was with great difficulty I got out of the water into Mr Heathcote's garden where I concealed myself for a short time in the garden house. When I made my escape out of the Guard Room I had no hat with me and my peruke being lost and my cloths wett I found myself very cold wich if I cou'd have bore, thought my situation far from safe and therefore determined of stripping of all my cloths leaving them in the garden house and swiming down the river wch I accordingly did for the space of abt 50 yards till I came to the Ware [weir] and from thence waded down the water for about 70 yards before I cou'd land on the other side which when I had done I ran down keeping close to the river side for near three miles and then discovered Alvaston, a village not far distant from but on the other side the river, and being extremely cold and almost spent out I resolv'd to make the best of my way thither which obliged me to swim again across the river. It was with great difficulty that I got to the town where I went to the back door of the first house that I came to which proved to be one Mr Rigley's where I was reced [received] and behav'd to with great humanity." [75]

By far the most interesting and controversial spy, however, at least by his own account, was the picaresque Irish adventurer Dudley Bradstreet. Bradstreet was born in Tipperary in 1711. He had spent a short time as a trooper in the cavalry and then tried his hand, unsuccessfully, first as a linen merchant and then as a brewer. Failing at both of these trades he lived for a number of years a chaotic lifestyle on the fringes of criminal society. In 1744, finding himself, as usual, somewhat strapped for cash, he offered his services to the government as a paid spy, and was able to persuade the Duke of Newcastle to pay him £100 on account of his expenses. Under his alias Oliver Williams, a reference to Oliver Cromwell and William III, he represented himself in Jacobite circles as a strong supporter of the Stuarts and a Stuart restoration. No doubt his Irish antecedents helped in the deception, although he was in fact from a Protestant rather than a Catholic family. According to Bradstreet's version of events, he arrived in Derby late in the evening of Thursday 5th December, just as Eleizer Birch was being interrogated at Exeter House, having left Lichfield, some 16 miles away, at 4 pm. On the way he stopped in an alehouse near Burton on Trent to drink with some rebel soldiers. On arriving in Derby he represented himself as a Jacobite gentleman who had come to offer his services and wished to meet the Prince. He says that he was accepted without reserve and immediately introduced to senior Jacobite commanders at Exeter House, including the Duke of Perth, Lord Kilmarnock and the Jacobite army's Adjutant General, the Irish soldier John William O'Sullivan. Here he told them that there was a strong government force of "eight or ten thousand men" at Northampton ready to meet the Jacobites as they marched south to London, while Cumberland with his "hussars and eight or nine thousand foot" prepared to cut off the Jacobite's retreat from his quarters at Lichfield. The army at Northampton was, of course, a complete figment of Bradstreet's imagination. He maintains that, having given this information to the Jacobite officers, he was then called into the council of war in an adjoining room, and repeated the information. This is his version taken from his memoirs:-

"in about five Minutes I was ushered in where they all sat in Council, and there asked the same Questions, and affirmed what was before related; when I came to that Part concerning an Army being at Northampton, the Rebel Prince, who was in a Closet just by, opened the

Door and pointed at me, saying, "That Fellow will do me more Harm than all the Elector's Army" and then directing himself to the Council, said, "You ruin, abandon, and betray me if you don't march on," and then shut the Door in a Passion. Sir Thomas Sheridan asked me, if I saw this Army at Northampton, or had it by Hearsay; I assured him I saw it, and again produced my Pass, which confirmed my having left London the Monday before, and that Northampton was my Road, and to put it out of all manner of Doubt, desired that they might send any body they could confide in, with my Pass and Name, by which means he might go to Northampton, and return again with Safety. This Proposal gaining me great Credit among them, then added, I never heard or read of a Man who for Lucre of Gain would scheme anything that must, to his certain Knowledge, end in a speedy and shameful Death, which I desired might be my Case if I deceived them, and desired at the same time to be closely kept till the Return of their Agent, and if he did not confirm what I said, would be contented to suffer instant Death, with their most curious Inventions of Torture; upon this they had entire Faith in my Report." [76]

In short, Bradstreet takes the whole credit for the decision of the council of war to retreat back to Scotland (see next chapter). His account appears to have been accepted in its entirety without question by many, but not all, historians of the period including Christopher Duffy ("The 45" - page 301) and FJ McLynn (The Jacobite Army in England 1745 - page 129). This is surprising. The story he tells is, one has to say, inherently improbable; it is highly unlikely that the Jacobites, who were intensely aware of the presence of spies in Derby and had only just arrested Eleizer Birch, would have taken Bradstreet at face value; who was this supposed Jacobite gentleman who had come forward at a very late stage, on his own, without credentials or followers and of whom none of them had ever heard? Bradstreet himself was a notorious liar and braggart with a long history of disreputable behaviour, and, as we now know, he wrote his memoir primarily to make money for himself because the government refused to pay him for his spying services after the rebellion was suppressed. Furthermore, not a single one of the eyewitnesses to the council of war mentions his presence. This is astonishing in itself, because such an intervention by a complete stranger, which tipped the balance of the decision in the council, would most certainly have merited a mention by at least one of the other participants. We can now provide, for the first time in a history of the Forty-Five, conclusive evidence that Bradstreet's account is a tissue of lies from start to finish. Dr Eveline Cruickshanks, the doyenne of modern

Jacobite studies, has researched this point in detail and has made a thorough examination of the relevant parts of the State Papers Domestic Series 36. She has very generously allowed me to use her unpublished results. In his account Bradstreet says that he accompanied the Jacobite army on their retreat as far as Preston where he left them, supposedly on a spying mission. Near Wigan he says that he met up with another Hanoverian agent, Edward Smalley, gave Smalley full particulars of what had occurred at Derby and, in effect, dictated a letter to be sent Bradstreet's paymaster, the Duke of Newcastle in London. In this lengthy letter no mention whatever is made of Bradstreet's contribution to the council of war at Derby, and if it had happened he would surely have mentioned it then. Over the next few months Bradstreet wrote a series of letters to Newcastle seeking payment for his services; nine of them are still extant, and the only one that mentions his role at Derby simply says "I am certain that my intelligence there was the cause of their retreat." Nothing at all is said about his supposed meeting with senior Jacobite officers or about his attendance at the council of war. There is little doubt that he went to Derby, as he claims, but it appears that he was detained there by suspicious Jacobites. He also, apparently, accompanied the retreating army as far as Preston, where he made his escape; what he certainly did not do was attend the council of war. [77]

In some ways it is rather sad to demolish this long-standing canard. Bradstreet was, like many rogues, a consummate raconteur and his version of what happened is dramatic and entertaining, but, alas, we can now say, beyond a reasonable doubt, that it is pure invention concocted a decade later to make more convincing his attempts to recover payment for his services from the government. However active the government's intelligence system was in Derby, we can now be certain that it was not the actions of a Hanoverian spy that caused the Jacobites to reach their fateful decision on Thursday 5th December 1745. How and why they did so will be the subject of the next chapter.

Chapter 9

The Council of War

There can be little doubt that the Prince and his army were elated to be in Derby after their long march from Edinburgh. They were within 98 miles of London as the crow flies. They had marched 200 miles from Carlisle into England having fired hardly a single shot, they had evaded every attempt to bring them to battle by the government forces, and the road to the capital was open. In London there was a degree of panic; in September there had been a run on the Bank of England which paid out its customers in sixpences in order to reduce the rate of outflow of its capital; King George was preparing to lead his troops at Finchley, as he had done at the Battle of Dettingen two years before, but was also taking prudent steps to flee into exile in Hanover if necessary, and some senior politicians were said to be re-considering their allegiance.

However, all was not as rosy as it appeared to be for the Pretender's army. They had suffered significant losses through desertion on the way; the army that left Edinburgh some 7,500 strong but was now, probably, down to no more than 5,500. Whilst the rank and file and the Prince were in a state of semi-euphoria, the Jacobite officers, some of whom had served with the French regular army and were hard-headed professionals, took a much more sober and realistic view of the army's position. They were a very long way from home, the optimism of the clansmen might soon evaporate under the weight of practical considerations, such as who should get in the harvest, and the plain fact of the matter was that their arrival in Derby, far from bringing in the hundreds of Jacobite supporters that agents such as Butler had suggested, had brought in a grand total of five recruits and none of them were of the gentry class who might be expected to have political influence and bring their followers with them. There is some suggestion that Welsh Jacobites under Sir Watkin Williams Wynn were about to march to the Prince's support. This is dealt with in greater detail in Chapter 12, but, in the event, it failed to materialise.

Clearly, therefore, there were important decisions to be made and to be made quickly. After the service at All Saints on the morning of Thursday 5th December, a council of war was convened at the Prince's lodgings at Exeter House. Present were the Prince himself, the Duke of Perth, Lord George Murray, Lord Elcho, Lord Balmerino, Sir Thomas Sheridan (the Prince's aged former tutor), John William

O'Sullivan, and the various colonels of the clan regiments including Cameron of Lochiel, MacDonald of Keppoch, MacDonald of Clanranald, John Roy Stewart, Ewan McPherson of Cluny and Charles Stewart of Ardshiel. Although we know what the final decision was, it is right to say that the course of the discussions is obscure; although there were several eyewitnesses to the debate, no single one of them agrees entirely with any of the others, so we have to construct a likely scenario as best we can. There are eight accounts that are, or purport to be, eyewitness: two versions by Lord Elcho, two by Lord George Murray and one each by Maxwell of Kirkconnell, John William O'Sullivan, the Chevalier Johnstone, and Prince Charles himself, written at a much later date in response to an enquiry sent to him in 1770. One of the Prince's two secretaries, John Hay of Restalrig denies that there was a council of war at all. He simply says:-

"Charles was just going out and had put on his bonnet, when Lord George Murray came in; and said to him, that it was high time to think what they were to do. Charles asked him what he meant, as he thought it was resolved to march on. Lord George said, that most of the Chiefs were of a different opinion, and thought they should march back to Ashbourne, and join the army from Scotland, which was believed to be following them fast - Charles was extremely offended, and absolutely averse to march back, since they had now so far carried their point as to have got before the Duke's army. Lord George Murray went and came, and used the names of many of the Chiefs, who, he said, were bent upon a junction with the other army. The whole day was spent in brigue and cabal, but no council of war was called." [78]

In the face of the other evidence we can safely discount this narrative of what occurred. Likewise there is a lively account by the Chevalier Johnstone which has frequently been quoted by historians. In it he states that, "The Duke of Perth alone took no part, at first, in these debates between the Prince and the chiefs of the clans, resting his head against the fireplace and listening to the dispute without uttering a single word; but at last he declared himself loudly of the opinion of the other chiefs." It would be nice to include this engaging pen portrait of the Duke of Perth, but, alas, the likelihood is that Johnstone was never present at the council. He had previously been the aide de camp to Lord George Murray and if he had still been in that position at Derby it is quite probable that he would have been in attendance with Murray at the Council; however, after the Battle of Prestonpans he relinquished his post, much to Lord George Murray's annoyance, and became a simple Captain in the Duke of Perth's regiment; in that capacity he would certainly not have been invited to the Council, so we can ignore his version as a genuine eyewitness account, although it is possible that he may have had the story from someone else who was present.

We can be reasonably certain of one thing, that the Prince and Lord George Murray entered the discussions with completely opposing views. The Prince, having come so far, was determined to push on for London in spite of the lack of support evinced by the population of the Midlands and North of England. The march so far had produced no more than 300 or so recruits, and none of any social standing apart from Col Francis Townley. Lord George, never wholly convinced by the invasion plans in the first place, had now been persuaded beyond doubt that the lack of English Jacobite support would be fatal to the Prince's prospects and that the only realistic decision would be a retreat to the Jacobite heartland in Scotland.

In the morning session of the council of war, which not all of the senior commanders attended (the Duke of Atholl and Lord Nairne, amongst others, were both absent), there was some agonised discussion about the lack of support from English Jacobites, and about the position and strength of the government forces under Cumberland, on their right flank, and Wade in their rear. It was suggested, possibly by Lord George himself, that defeat of the Jacobite army would bring down the militia on the remnants:-

"...Upon a misfortune it could not be supposed one man could escape, for the militia, who had not appeared much against us hitherto, would upon our defeat possess all the roads and the Enemy's Horse would surround us on all hands. the whole world would blame us as being rash and foolish to venture a thing that could not succeed, and the Prince's person, should he escape being killed in battle, must fall into the enemy's hands." [79]

Concern was expressed lest a defeat of the Jacobites result in the capture of the Prince, but Charles was adamant that a forward march to London was the only course and started to give directions as to the order of march for the following day. At this point Lord George Murray intervened and gives a reasoned account of his position in his unpublished papers, referring to himself in the third person as was common at the time:-

".... Lord George Murray said that he believed the first thing to be spoke of was how far it was prudent to advance any further. His Royal Highness turned to some of the other officers who also said that they did not see how they could extricate themselves out of so imminent a danger, for that their hopes of a French landing or a powerful junction in England had failed. The Prince seem'd thunder-struck - as if they were against his obtaining a victory and a certain Restoration. He expressed himself as convinced of both.

At last Lord George Murray, seeing the uneasiness of everybody, desired leave to represent his thoughts upon so critical a juncture. Tho' he had not talked with any of the officers upon it, yet he now thought himself obliged to declare his opinion expressly as by what he observed most of the officers seemed to expect it. He said he was as desirous to see a happy Restoration as any man in Britain. He was ready to sacrifice his life and his all whenever there was an occasion. Tho' they were at present in a very dangerous situation, yet he hoped it was not desperate. If they went on another day it was not possible to save His Royal Highness. Both his life and all those brave men with him must be inevitably sacrificed. Suppose he should even beat the Duke of Cumberland, it would cost him the lives of a great many of his best men. He would not advance his affairs by it for the remains of the Duke of Cumberland's army would join the other which was still betwixt him and London - especially the Horse. The other army, if they thought they had not him secure enough, would by lining the hedges, by cannon, or other impediments retard his march and kill many of his people. By that time General Wade would come up and join the others and so surround his army and either kill or take everyone prisoner. Even supposing he could shun fighting with the last two armies he would be so disabled by the loss from fighting the first that he would make but a poor figure with the remains of his army should he get to London." [80]

Lord Elcho gives some support to Lord George Murray's version in his Narrative:-

" The 5(th) in the morning Lord George Murray and all the Commanders of the Battalions and Squadrons waited upon the Prince, and Lord George told him that it was the opinion of Every body present that the Scots had now done all that could be Expected of them. That they had marched into the heart of England ready to join any party that would declare for him, that none had, and that the Counties through which the Army had pass'd had Seemed much more Enemies than friends to his Cause, that there was no French Landed in England, and that if their was any party in England, it was very odd that they had never so much as Either sent him money or intelligence or the least advice what to do, but if he Could produce any letter from any person of distinction in which their [sic] was an invitation for the army to go to London, or to any other part of England, that they were ready to go. But if nobody had either invited them or meddled in the least of their affairs, it was to be Supposed that their [sic] was either no party at all, or if their [sic] was they did not chuse to act with them, or else they would ere now have lett them know it. Suppose even the Army march'd on and beat the Duke of Cumberland yett in the Battle they must Lose some men, and they had after that the King's own army consisting of 7,000 men near London to deal with. On the contrary, if either of these armies beat them, their [sic] would not a Man escape, as the militia, altho they durst never face the army while in a body, yett they would have courage enough to putt an end to them if ever they were routed." [81]

James Maxwell of Kirkconnel, one of the Prince's aides de camp, and a Captain in the Prince's Lifeguards, corroborates these accounts:-

"When the Council met next morning, Lord George Murray represented to the Prince and his Councillors that they had marched so far into England depending upon French succours, or an insurrection in the country, neither of which had happened; that the Prince's army, by itself, was by no means a match for the troops the Elector of Hanover had got together; that, besides Wade's army, that was coming up in the rear, and was ten thousand strong, and the Duke of Cumberland's, which was in front, and was said to consist of between seven and eight thousand, there was a third army forming about London, and that the smallest of the three exceeded the Prince's army in numbers, and they were all veteran troops; that suppose the Prince should beat the first of these armies he should engage, he might be undone by a victory; should he lose a thousand or fifteen hundred of his best men, the rest would be altogether unfit to engage a fresh army, which must happen a few days after." [82]

At some stage in the proceedings, the Prince's Secretary of State, John Murray of Broughton, inadvertently entered the room while the council was in session and, in his later deposition, taken after he surrendered and turned King's evidence, said:-

"... he offered to go back, but the Pretender called him into the Room, and told him, in some heat, that he was quite scandalised, for that they were pressing him to go back to Scotland, instead of marching directly to London as had been intended. That they, Lord George Murray, Lord Elcho, and every Body present, except Lord Perth, declared their opinion for marching back to Scotland. that the Pretender insisted to go on to London, but at last yielded to the opinion of the Council of War (as this Examinant [i.e. Murray of Broughton] advised him to do), and it was resolved to march back to Scotland."[83]

Discussion became heated, at one stage swords were drawn, and by lunchtime the council of war had been adjourned, no doubt to let tempers cool and to give the parties time to reflect on the arguments that had been deployed in the morning. However, the gist of what had passed clearly got out and was badly received by some senior Jacobites who had not been present. The elderly, choleric and alcoholic Sir John Macdonald, who had come over with the Prince, gives details of his own reaction in his memoirs:-

"Next day there was a council held, at which, against the opinion of the Duke of Atholl, of Clan Ranald, and of the Duke of Perth (but I don't think he was there, being excluded on account of his religion) it was decided to right about turn, and return to Scotland. I was quickly informed of this and sought the Councillors, and found in one room, Lochiel, Capoch [Keppoch], Sheridan and Lord George. Taking no notice of the last named, I addressed myself to Lochiel and said to him that I was much astonished that such a gallant fellow as he was, at the head of a troop of brave followers, should think of turning back - that I was very sure that his Camerons like the Macdonalds would follow the Prince to London, that it was absurd to think of making such a long retreat with an undisciplined force like ours, in the face of regular troops in their own country; that if we were to perish, it were better to do so with our faces to London than to Scotland. He answered me that there were many deserters and that 'if you knew all, you would agree with us' His reasons seemed to me so weak and I was so angry that I left the room in haste." [84]

This account is confirmed by Lord George's own laconic comment that "This gentleman was old and had dined heartily, for he was much subject to the bottle."

While the council of war was adjourned, what was the Prince doing? One intriguing suggestion was that he occupied part of the day by visiting the heads of some prominent local families with supposed Jacobite sympathies in order to try and persuade them to join the rising and thus give some support to the Prince's position in the council; with the accession of some families of standing and their followers, he could attempt to give the lie to Lord George Murray's vehemently expressed view that a march to London was doomed without substantial support from English Jacobites.

Some sources have suggested that, on his march from Ashbourne, the Prince visited German Pole of Radbourne, a prominent local Tory who had stood for Parliament in the by-election in Derby in 1742. This was first raised by the Rev. J. C. Cox in his book "Three Centuries of Derbyshire Annals" in which he says (without citing any authorities):-

"Evidence reached us some years ago from two different sources that we cannot doubt (for in each case the tradition has only passed through two people, and was supplied by those who had received it from their grandfathers who were present), that Prince Charles Edward, on December 4th, when marching from Ashbourne to Derby, turned aside for an hour or two at Mr German Pole's of Radbourne, where he met by previous secret arrangement several of the leading recusants (Catholics) of Derbyshire, Leicestershire and Staffordshire, as well as representatives of other families. Mr German Pole was not himself a recusant, though of strong Jacobite tendencies, but was a connection of the well-known Poles of Spinkhill, and others of his own branch of the family were Romanists. Our information leads us to believe that the Prince here made up his own mind that retreat was necessary before ever he had entered Derby, one of the reasons being the non-arrival of a large sum of money which was to have met him here from the Jacobites in Leicestershire and the south midlands, and which was afterwards coolly appropriated by the Derbyshire yeoman entrusted with its custody." [85]

We can certainly discount the last part of the statement. The Prince had no intention whatever of retreating back to Scotland at this stage and, indeed, as we have seen, argued strongly against it on the following morning during the first session of the council. At all events, around this bald statement, unsupported by any authorities, Eardley

Simpson, in his book "Derby and the Forty-five" published in 1933, wove an entire narrative about the Prince's contacts with local families while he was in Derby. The likelihood of this was the subject of considerable controversy at the time and can never be proved with any degree of probability but it is of sufficient interest to include here. Simpson suggests that, in the interval between the sittings of the council, the Prince, possibly accompanied by German Pole of Radbourne, visited Sir Robert Burdett at Foremark Hall and Sir Henry Harpur at Calke Abbey and that the former two, accompanied by the Prince, may then have ridden on to Nether Hall which may have been the family home of Lord Mountjoy, another supposed Jacobite supporter mentioned in Butler's list. It has proved impossible to show that Mountjoy lived at Nether Hall, although his family name was Blount and the hall is very close to the village of Barton Blount, so on that very tenuous evidence it is possible, but unlikely. All that we can say is that the Prince may well have tried to persuade local Tories to join him. He had certainly used his considerable personal charm in this way in Scotland, visiting some of the clan chiefs to win them over and succeeding. In Derbyshire, if it happened at all, his charisma clearly proved unequal to the task. [86]

Later in the day the council was re-convened. It is clear that whatever efforts the Prince had made in the meantime to attract support from putative local Jacobite supporters had been wholly unsuccessful, but he was still, seemingly, determined to advance his view that the march on London should be continued, come what may. How much support he had in this from the other members of the council is unclear. It has been suggested that the Duke of Atholl, who had not been present at the morning session, was initially in favour of continuing, but was easily dissuaded by the arguments of the opposing side, particularly when those in favour of the march on London refused to confirm their opinions in writing. Lord George Murray deals with his elder brother's views in his account:-

"The Duke of Atholl seemed much for going forward. In the evening when this was understood by the rest of the officers, they told his Royal Highness that they valued their lives as little as brave men ought to do, and if he inclined to go forward they would do their duty to the last, but desired that those who advised his Royal Highness to go forward would sign their opinion, which would be a great satisfaction to them. This put a stop to all underhand dealings, and the Duke of Atholl when he heard others upon the subject was fully satisfied as to the necessity of the measure." [87]

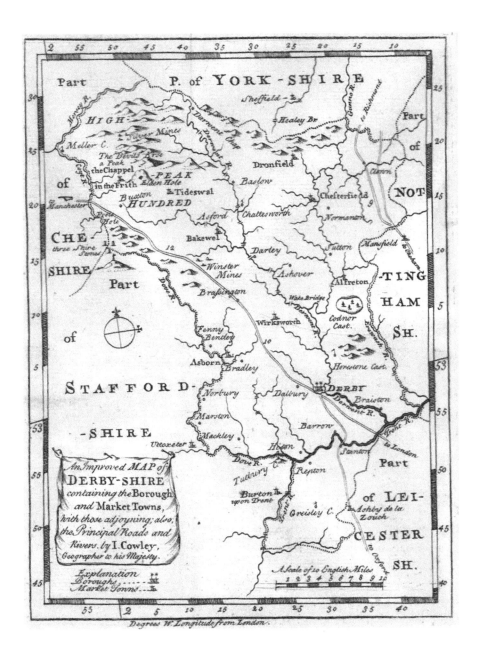

1. Derbyshire in 1744

2. King James III, the "Old Pretender", father of
Bonnie Prince Charlie
(author's collection)

3. Bonnie Prince Charlie as a Child,
c. 1737 (author's collection)

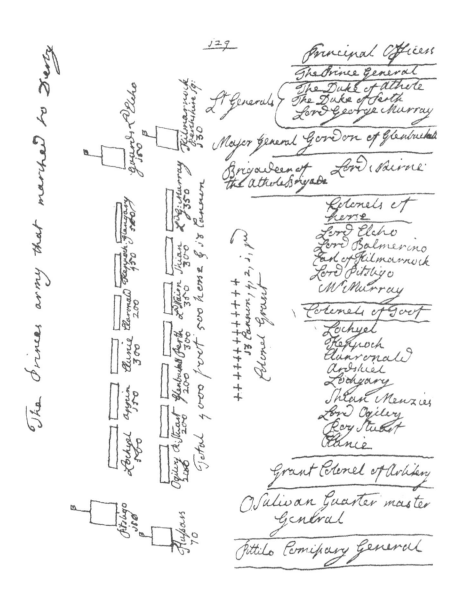

**4. A plan made by Lord Elcho of the Highland
Army that marched to Derby
(author's collection)**

5. A highland "targe" (shield) left behind at the Meynell town house by the Highland Army in 1745.

6. The mortar left behind at Derby by the Jacobite Army on their retreat, now at Kedleston Hall

7. The notice attached to the mortar giving details of its provenance.

8. The Meynell town house, Derby, requisitioned for Lord Pitsligo

9. Bingham's House, Derby, requisitioned for Lord Nairne

10. The George Inn, Derby (now Mr. Jorrocks pub) where the Duke of Devonshire raised the Derbyshire Blues regiment

11. Plaque at the Mr. Jorrocks pub commemorating
the Duke of Devonshire's raising

12. Swarkestone Bridge, the furtherst point reached
by the rebel army

13. The Swarkestone cairn, marking the furthest point south

14. The Bonnie Prince Charlie statue, Full Street, Derby,
Adjacent to where Exeter House once stood

15. The Bonnie Prince Charlie Room, Derby Museum
with panelling rescued from Exeter House

Maison à Derby, dans laquelle logea le Prétendant:

**16. Exeter House, Derby, demolished in 1854
(author's collection)**

**17. Plaque in Derbys Cathedral commemorating the service held by the
Jacobites on 5th. December, 1745**

Times of Public Diſtreſs Times of Trial.

BEING THE

SUBSTANCE

OF SOME

SERMONS

Preach'd in the

TRON-CHURCH of *Edinburgh,*

In the Month of *November,* 1745.

On Occaſion of the

Preſent Rebellion.

By GEORGE WISHART, *M. A.*
One of the Miniſters of EDINBURGH.

L O N D O N:

Printed for A. MILLAR, oppoſite *Katharine Street*
in the *Strand*; and ſold by M. COOPER, at the
Globe in *Pater-noſter Row.* MDCCXLVI.

18. The front page of *Some Sermons Preach'd.. On Occasion of the*
Present Rebellion

The London Gazette

EXTRAORDINARY.

𝔓𝔲𝔟𝔩𝔦𝔰𝔥𝔢𝔡 𝔟𝔶 𝔄𝔲𝔱𝔥𝔬𝔯𝔦𝔱𝔶.

THURSDAY, *December* 12, 1745.

Derby, December 8.

THE Rebels behaved tolerably well in their March Southwards, but have plundered the Country in their Retreat. Many of the best Houses here have suffered. Two of them were taken with their Arms, between Ashbourn and Derby, by a Farmer and two Boys, and were sent to the Camp at Meriden Common. In this Town they demanded Billets for 10,000 Men, but those who computed their Numbers as exactly as possible assure us, that they did not exceed Six thousand three hundred Horse and Foot. The Horse were extremely jaded, and in a bad Condition. In the Number above were many old Men, and Boys of fifteen and sixteen Years of Age, all without Shoes and Stockings.

Coventry, Dec. 9. The Rebels were at Ashbourn on Saturday Morning, and went to Leek that Night. Before they left Ashbourn they shot two Men, one of whom died on the Spot. They have taken all the Horses they could lay their Hands upon, and have plundered and done great Damage. They had 15 Pieces of Cannon, and one Mortar.

Mansfield, Dec. 9. By an Express just arrived from Leek there is an Account, that 1000 of the Rebels marched last Night from thence for Macclesfield, and that at Six this Morning the main Body began to march the same Way, and their Artillery at Eight.

Stafford, Dec. 9. The Van Guard of the Rebels was in Manchester Yesterday, and their main Body at Macclesfield.

Warrington, Dec. 10. By a Messenger sent out of this Town to observe the Motions of the Rebels we hear, that their Foot and Baggage passed by Pendleton Pole, which is one Mile from Manchester, this Morning, and took the Road which leads to Leigh, Wigan and Preston. The same Messenger informs us, that he was told the Horse designed to stay in Manchester all Night; but we have since heard, that their whole Body have left Manchester, and taken the above Road.

Litchfield, Dec. 11. We have Advices here, that the Rebels left Manchester Yesterday, marching Northwards; and that his Royal Highness the Duke of Cumberland had made two forc'd Marches after them, and continued in Pursuit of them.

[Price Two-pence.]

---

19. A page from the London Gazette describing the retreat from Derby

20. Lord Elcho, senior Jacobite commander and present at the Council of War on 5th. December, 1745

21. William Augustus, Duke of Cumberland, commander of the
Government forces in December 1745

22. *The Army marching to Finchley,* an engraving after William Hogarth
(author's collection)

23. The Jacobite Rose (see appendix 10) (author's collection)

24. A collection of contemporary Jacobite medals (author's collection)

25. Re-enactment of the '45 in Derby – two members of the
Manchester Regiment

Some historians have taken the position that the Scots clan chiefs and the other Scots members of the Council, led by Lord George Murray, were for retreat, whilst the Irish members, including the Adjutant General John William O'Sullivan, were for marching on; interestingly, however, O'Sullivan's own, eccentrically spelled, account refers to his support for a retreat as early as Manchester. Of his part in the council he says:-

"The Chiefs & others were sent for, who were the most part of them for the retraite, and really according to all the rulles of War, & prudence, it was the only party [i.e.decision] to be taken (Sullivan propos'd it at Manchester finding yt not a man of any consequence appear'd) but a Young Prince, yt sees himself within three days, or at utmost four days, march of the Capital, where if he was once arrived, wou'd in all appearance restor the King, cou'd not relish the word of retrait, & really he wou'd not hear yt word from the beginning, he had an avertion to the word it self, but finding every body allmost of yt oppinion was oblidged to consent." [88]

Lord Elcho makes clear in his Narrative that the Prince continued vehement in his views and that the sessions were stormy:-

"The Prince heard all these arguments with the greatest impatience, fell into a passion, and gave most of the Gentlemen that had Spoke very Abusive language, and said that they had a mind to betray him. The Case was, he knew nothing about the country nor had the Smallest Idea of the force that was against him, nor where they were Situated......He Continued all that day positive he would march to London.....at Night the Prince sent for them and told them he consented to go to Scotland. And at the same time he told them that for the future he would have no more Councills, for he would neither ask nor take their Advice, that he was Accountable to nobody for his Actions but to his Father, and he was as good as his word, for he never after advised with any body but the Irish Officers, Mrs Murray & [John] Hay [of Restalrig], and never more summons'd a Councill." [89]

Perhaps we should leave the last word with the Prince himself. Many years later, in 1775, the historian of the rising John Home, wrote to the Prince in Rome asking him what had happened at the council. Charles' reply was brief and to the point.

"M. le Comte [i.e. Charles] affirms that the retreat of the army was in consequence of a council of war held in his presence some time before the retreat took place, composed of the General officers and Chiefs; and that all the members except M. le Comte himself, were of opinion that the retreat was absolutely necessary; and that M. le Comte endeavoured to persuade some of them to join with him, but could not prevail upon a single person." [90]

This summary, by the Prince himself, albeit many years later, seems to provide conclusive evidence of what happened at the council, and there is no reason to doubt that it is a truthful and accurate statement of what occurred.

After the decision was made, it seems that the Prince may have decided to hold a ball or rout for his local supporters. This could have been at the Virgin Inn on the corner of Full Street and the Market Place or at the Assembly Rooms in Full Street which had been built in 1714 (they would be replaced by new and bigger Assembly Rooms in 1763). More likely, however, is that he simply allowed his supporters to come to Exeter House to bid him farewell. John Daniel, who had joined the Prince's army at Garstang during the march to Manchester, noted in his journal a disturbing omen that occurred:-

"Great numbers of People and Ladies (who had come from afar to see the Prince), crowding into his room, overturned a table, which in falling overturned and broke the Royal Standard soon after our return was agreed upon so I leave the reader to judge and make his reflexions on this. It would seem certain at least that Providence miraculously concurs, while such and such things are carried on. Thus, when Moses held up his hands, Joshua prevailed; but when through weariness he in the least relaxed the Israelites had the worst of it. So perhaps it was, that our enterprise was not vigorously enough pursued: and remarkable it certainly was, that the Royal Standard should be broken immediately after our return was resolved upon." [91]

Chapter 10

The Retreat

The news that the army was to retreat back to Scotland came as an enormous blow to the rank and file, particularly in the clan regiments, whose long, and virtually unopposed, march into England had convinced them that they had only to unleash one more highland charge on the Hanoverian army and the capital, and hence the country, would be theirs. They had spent the previous day in preparing their weapons in anticipation of a battle with Cumberland's army on the following day. Consequently, in order not to affect their morale, word was given out that the army was, in fact, advancing to meet the enemy. Maxwell of Kirkconnel chronicled the effect on the highlanders when the position became clear:-

"The retreat was begun on the 6th. To conceal it from the enemy as long as possible, a party of horse was ordered to advance some miles towards them, while the army took the road to Ashborn; and to keep the army in suspense, powder and ball were distributed as before an action, and it was insinuated that Wade was at hand, and they were going to fight him; but when the soldiers found themselves on the road to Ashborn, they began to suspect the truth, and seemed extremely dejected. All had expressed the greatest ardour upon hearing at Derby that they were within a day's march of the Duke of Cumberland; they were at a loss what to think of this retreat, of which they did not know the real motives; but even such as knew them, and thought the retreat the only reasonable scheme, could hardly be reconciled to it. When it was question of putting it in practice, another artifice was thought of to amuse them. It was given out that the reinforcements expected from Scotland were on the road, and had already entered England; that Wade was endeavouring to intercept them, and the Prince was marching to their relief; that as soon as they had joined him, he would resume his march to London. This pretext was plausible....The hopes of returning immediately made them somewhat easy under their present disappointment, but still all was sullen and silent that whole day." [92]

Some of the rank and file were in a mutinous state. Duncan Stuart, a private in John Roy Stuart's Edinburgh Regiment, "..near Ashburne threw down his gun in sight of the regiment and said he would go no farther (whereupon he had a guard set over him for a few hours).." [93]

In order to deceive the enemy, the Prince and the army left Derby by a circuitous route. According to the Vicar of All Saint's, the Reverend Henry Cantrell:-

"On Friday morning at nine o'clock, their Prince, being well mounted, set out from my Lord Exeter's house, went over the Market Place, up the Rotten Row and down the Sadler's Gate on the way to Ashbourne." [94]

Parties of horse were sent out from Swarkestone Bridge towards Loughborough and ordered to double back later and join the main army. According to the *London Gazette*:-

"This morning early, several parties of the Highland horse were in motion in the roads about Derby. Some of them seemed to be moving towards Loughborough, others kept on the Ashbourne side, at ten the whole returned to Derby and then set out for Ashbourne. The horse moved first, soon afterwards passed their artillery, consisting of thirteen pieces of cannon, and then their main body of foot."

In fact we have details of the order of march from Lord Ogilvy's Order Book. It was as follows:-

Life Guards - **The Van**
Kilmarnock's Horse
Atholl Brigade (with the Royal Standard)
Perth's Regiment
Ogilvy's Regiment
The Edinburgh Regiment
Glenbucket's Regiment
Manchester Regiment
Artillery and Baggage Train
Glengarry's Regiment
Clanranald's Regiment
Keppoch's Regiment
Appin Regiment
Cameron of Lochiel's Regiment
Cluny MacPherson's Regiment
Pitsligo's Horse
Bagot's Hussars - **The Rear Guard**

The password for the day was "John and Bristol" (to give the impression that the army was still southward bound) and an officer from each regiment was to accompany Pitsligo's Horse in order to collect any stragglers. [95]

Clearly the Prince's morale was very badly affected by the decision, and no doubt, in his own mind, he had already decided that the rising was doomed to failure. On the way down through England he had marched jauntily and tirelessly at the head of his army and had been up each morning early to prepare for the day's affairs. On the morning of the retreat, Black Friday as it became known to Jacobites, he rose late and did not leave Derby until about 9 am, thus compelling the rearguard, under Lord George Murray, to delay their departure for longer than was prudent. In fact the last remnants did not leave the town until nearly midday. Lord Elcho commented on the change in the Prince's behaviour:- "the Prince, who had march'd all the way to Darby on foot at the head of a Column of Infantry, now mounted on horseback, and road generally after the van of the Army and appear'd to be out of humour" and John Hay of Restalrig also noted the poor morale of the army and the terrible psychological change in the Prince's demeanour that had been wrought by the stresses and strains of the previous day:-

"Next morning when they began their march, very few knew that they were marching back: many persons of distinction did not know it; amongst others Lord Nairne. When the men, who had marched in the grey of the morning, began to know by day-light, from the marks they taken of the road, that they were going back, there was an universal lamentation amongst them. Charles, who had marched a-foot at the head of the men all the way, was obliged to get on horseback, for he could not walk, and hardly stand (as was always the way with him when he was cruelly used)." [96]

Lord George Murray observed:-

"His Royal Highness, in marching forwards, had always been the first up in the morning, and had the men in motion before the break of day, and commonly marched himself afoot; but in the retreat he was much longer in leaving his quarters, so that though the rest of the army were all on their march, the rear could not move till he went, and then he rode straight on and got to the quarters with the van." [97]

Sir John MacDonald, the inebriated septuagenarian Jacobite officer who objected so strongly to the decision of the council of war noted:-

"The following morning the army faced round and marched by the same route it had come, the Highlanders in great affliction and somewhat disorderly; many of the officers even going ahead to secure good lodgings, and the common soldiers scattered over the country, a few even were killed by the country people". [98]

As the Prince was leaving Derby, the Duke of Perth and his aide de camp went to Alderman Heathcote's house with pistols drawn and cocked seeking the escaped spy Eleizer Birch who Heathcote was suspected of hiding. Birch, of course, had already made good his escape and was being looked after in Alvaston some three miles away.

On the march down, the Prince's army had been relatively well-behaved and there were few instances of looting and disorder, other than the normal requisitioning of food and forage and the usual levying of a money subscription from each town. On the way back, however, it was a different story. The *Gentleman's Magazine* gave details:-

"Letters from Derby, dated December 8, say that the rebels behaved tolerably well in the march Southwards, but plundered the country in their retreat; that many of the best houses there had suffered; that two of the rebels were taken with their arms between Ashburn and Derby by a farmer and two boys, and sent to the camp at Meriden common......before they left Ashburn they shot two men, one of whom died on the spot. They took all the horses they could lay their hands on, and plundered and did great damage." [99]

At Okeover Hall (residence of the Okeover family since the 10th century), a contingent of cavalry (probably Bagot's Hussars), plundered the hall of everything of value. The chaplain, German Kitching, wrote an anguished letter about it to the squire, Leak Okeover:-

"We have had a dreadful time ye last week; upon Tuesday night we had five lay with us, and upon Friday night as they return'd from Derby four lay with us and about Seven a Clock came six Horsemen and said they wanted Armour and plunder'd ye House and Stables and Barns and ye Church; they have taken your best Saddle trimm'd with Gold Lace and ye Furniture belonging to it and your Lady's bridle and two other Saddles and two other Bridles and two pair of Boots - and upon Tuesday a young mare and upon Saturday morning a Grey pad both at Christopher Tomlinsons and they have taken all your Horses at Okeover. We kept out of their way and sav'd them all - upon Saturday morning after they was gone came Three Ruffians and said they wanted money and took from me Eighteen Pence and pick yr Servants Pockets of their money and my Silver Tobacco Box: they kill'd none of us but threatened us much." [100]

Lord Ogilvy's Regimental Order Book makes two references to the hanging of offenders for looting, and at Mayfield, on the march from Ashbourne to Leek, the landlord of an inn was shot dead in an argument with highlanders, no doubt over the bill, and Humphrey Brown, a farmer at Clifton near Ashbourne, met the same fate for refusing to give up his horse. According to John Daniel a young Englishman in the Prince's army, presumably a member of the Manchester regiment, was murdered by a woman and her son:-

"A young English lad, who had joined the Prince, being somewhat before the army, had through weariness laid himself down to rest under a hedge, and fallen fast asleep. He was soon perceived by a woman and her boy: this cruel fiend immediately determined to murder him as he lay sleeping like a lamb, conscious of no harm; she accordingly with the assistance of her son cut the poor young man's throat. The army coming up soon after, we espied the mangled body in that shocking condition; and on searching the next house adjacent, we found a young boy in bed much besmeared with blood, and trembling, who confessed the fact, and said that his mother was the chief author of it. They were both taken into custody, and a report of the whole made to the Prince: but he was against their being put to death, so that by a wonderful clemency they escaped the just reward of their crime." [101]

There were other atrocities as well, on both sides. In Leek a highland straggler was brought before the local magistrate who ordered him to be shot and then flayed. A party of highlanders returned and castrated the magistrate in revenge. As can be imagined, there was much joy in the county at the departure of the highland army. Our old friend James Clegg, recorded his relief in his diary on 10th December:-"The Rebels are all returned to Manchester, they took several persons with them from Stockport. Blessed be God the silk mill is safe." [102]

The prince lodged on the Friday night at the house of a Mr Mills on the road between Leek and Buxton, and on the following day the army marched on to Macclesfield which they reached on the Saturday evening, observed by a local, John Stafford, who recorded that:-

"The Mayor and many of the inhabitants fled....1,500 at least came in about 5 or 6 on the Saturday evening......the town was very thin of Inhabitants and very dismal were the countenances of those who were left in it. the only comfort [was] to find the Rebels lookt full as dismal themselves. The main body came in soon after....and the Pretender's son was amongst 'em on horseback with a guard of about 40 and seemed to be in a good deal of a hurry". [103]

By 9th December the Jacobite vanguard had begun to enter Manchester. On the way Lord Elcho's men had been involved in an exchange of fire near Stockport with the newly emboldened militia, encouraged by the retreat of the rebels. The highlanders, in response, burned a number of houses. In Manchester itself the highlanders encountered much hostility, a discouraging experience after the joyful acclamation that they had received on the march south. A local report says:-

"The bellman (town crier) had been about the town on Sunday 8th December, to order all persons to provide pickaxes, etc to spoil the road, and again, to arm themselves with such weapons as they could get; and there were, 'tis believed, of the country and the town's folks about 10,000 soon collected, armed with scythes, hedgestakes, etc who seemed very hearty to have a brush with the rebels. But the Gentlemen considering, that, if they did stop them, it must be attended with the loss of a great many useful lives, and the hazard of the town being burnt, the bellman was sent about the town to order them to disperse......next day at noon, about 40 of the rebels came in. Several stones were thrown at them by the mob as they came thro' Hanging ditch. They threatened to fire but did not; and sat on horseback, some with pistols, others with guns in their hands, all ready cocked, till the main body came in. They billeted themselves most at their old quarters. They behaved worse than they did before." [104]

Gone were the "loud huzzas", the white cockades and bonfires; many of the recruits that had made up the Manchester Regiment appear to have deserted; only 113 were left to garrison Carlisle out of a total strength of between two and three hundred. There was even an attempted assassination of the Prince when the Jacobite Adjutant General John William O'Sullivan was fired on from a window in the town having been mistaken for the Prince.

The romantic Elizabeth Byrom, who had welcomed the Prince with open arms on his journey south, now gave a much more sober assessment of the return of the Jacobite army:-

"....about two o'clock they brought us word that a party of them was come in, and some people had slutched 'em and thrown stones, and so it proved; but the Highlanders told them, if they did not give over they must fire amongst them, so they gave over. I came home from my uncle's and met all the artillery going up and all the army coming in, and everybody went to their old quarters; the officers walked up and down the streets to send people to their own houses, and then the bellman went...that he [the Prince] orders no two persons be seen walking together in the streets at after nine o'clock tonight, except they be guarded by some of H R H own troops, on pain of being deemed mobbers and rioters and by them be punished as such." [105]

Having levied a fine on the town of £5,000, subsequently reduced to £2,500, the Prince's army marched on to Preston which they reached on 11th December, resting there for a day, and by 14th December they had reached Lancaster. The following day the highlanders began enter Kendal... This little lakeland town had always been hostile to the rebels, even on the way south, and now, as the vanguard entered the main street they were fired upon and two of Bagot's Hussars were killed. The highlanders fired back and killed two locals, and it was only the intervention of the Duke of Perth that prevented a wholesale massacre. On 16th December the Jacobites began to leave, but their rapid marches were now impeded by the difficult terrain and the Prince's insistence that all the artillery and baggage be taken with them. This caused Lord George Murray in the rearguard immense problems as he struggled to convey the heavy bronze guns up Shap Fell, and the pace of the highland army's march slowed to a crawl.

In the meantime, by dint of hard marching, Cumberland's army had managed to get within a few miles of the retreating Jacobites and by the morning of 18th December he had even managed to get a strong force of Dragoons in front of the Jacobite rearguard. A brisk skirmish ensued near the little village of Clifton, in which the

MacDonalds of Glengarry and the MacPhersons particularly distinguished themselves, the government forces losing perhaps forty killed and wounded to the Jacobites' dozen. This skirmish has the distinction of being the very last skirmish fought on English soil.

On the following day the army reached Carlisle. They had left a small garrison there on their way down and now, rather surprisingly, decided to leave a larger garrison as the rest of the army retreated into Scotland. The remnants of the Manchester Regiment, and some 300 men from other non-clan regiments were chosen for this impossible task. Within a week Cumberland's army had besieged and taken the town and with it the garrison; many of them were doomed to be executed or transported to the sugar cane plantations in Barbados, in itself the equivalent of a death sentence. By 20th December the Jacobite army was back over the Scottish border that they had crossed just six dramatic weeks previously, and the Prince's attempt to overthrow the Hanoverian regime was effectively at an end. It would now be only a matter of time before the rebels were crushed and the last embers of the rebellion extinguished.

Chapter 11

Aftermath

The Jacobites found their crossing of the River Esk at Longton much more difficult on the retreat than they had on the march south; the weather had deteriorated markedly, the winter of 1745 to 1746 was one of the most severe that there had been for many years, and the river was desperately cold and in spate. The army managed to cross under the protection of the Jacobite cavalry which entered the water and formed a line across the river to act as a breakwater. Nevertheless, several men and camp-followers were drowned, and the infantry were cold and exhausted by the time they gained the opposite bank. Having no fuel to light fires they danced vigorously to get the circulation back in their frozen limbs and to dry off their soaking plaids.

They marched on, sullen and depressed reaching Dumfries on 21st December, a town that had always been hostile to the Stuarts and was described as being "full of fanatical Calvinists". By Christmas Day they had reached Glasgow, perhaps the most Whiggish and pro-government town in Scotland. The Prince and his men were received with sullen hostility. As the highlanders approached, the Glasgow Regiment of militia, some 600 in number, followed the example of their colleagues in the Derbyshire Blues and retreated rapidly the 40 miles to Edinburgh which had been recaptured after the departure of the main Jacobite army for England. After forcing the authorities to provide 6,000 coats, bonnets, and pairs of shoes, together with 12,000 shirts, under threat of the city being sacked, the Prince held a muster of his army on Glasgow Green on 30th December. By this time he had been joined by Lord John Drummond with 4,000 of the 6,000 men available in the north east of Scotland, including some French regular troops which had successfully run the Royal Navy's blockade and had landed in Montrose the previous month. This brought the total of the Prince's forces up to about 10,000 men.

The retreat from England had left the Jacobite army in limbo, without any clear strategic purpose to their campaign, and this irresolution clearly shows over the ensuing months. By mid-January 1746 they were massed in the Central Lowlands, and on 17th January met the forces of General Henry Hawley at Falkirk. It was what soldiers call an "encounter battle". Both sides were taken by surprise when meeting the other as they were climbing opposite sides of Falkirk Muir. The Jacobite army numbered about 7,000 men and the government forces about 8,000. The battle began at about 3.30 in the afternoon, just as dusk was falling. Neither side had any artillery. Hawley's guns had become bogged down in the approach to the battlefield, and the Jacobite guns were deployed in a desultory siege of Stirling Castle, conducted by the wholly incompetent Chief Engineer Mirabelle de Gordon.

The action opened with a charge of the government dragoons against the Jacobite right wing which was composed of the Clan Donald Regiments. Initially the attack seemed to be successful, but the highlanders put up a ferocious and obstinate defence, dramatically described by the Chevalier de Johnstone:-

"The English began the attack with a body of about eleven hundred cavalry, who advanced very slowly against the right of our army, and did not halt till they were within twenty paces of our first line, to induce us to fire, The Highlanders, who had been particularly enjoined not to fire till the army was within musket-length of them, discharged their muskets the moment the cavalry halted and killed about eighty men, each of them having aimed at a rider. The commander of this body of cavalry, who had advanced some paces before his men, was of the number. The cavalry closing their ranks, which were opened by our discharge, put spurs to their horses and rushed upon the Highlanders at a hard trot, breaking their ranks, throwing down everything before them and trampling the Highlanders under the feet of their horses. The most singular and extraordinary combat immediately followed. The Highlanders, stretched on the ground, thrust their dirks into the bellies of the horses. Some seized riders by their clothes, dragged them down and stabbed them with their dirks, several again used their pistols, but few of them had sufficient space to use their swords. Macdonald of Clanranald, chief of one of the clans of the Macdonalds, assured me that whilst he was lying upon the ground under a dead horse which had fallen upon him, without the power of extricating himself, he saw a dismounted horseman struggling with a Highlander. Fortunately for him, the Highlander, being the strongest, threw his antagonist, and having killed him with his dirk, he came to his assistance and drew him with difficulty from under his horse." [106]

The defeat of the government cavalry was followed immediately by a charge of the Jacobite centre which broke through the ranks of the redcoats opposite and would have swept them entirely from the field if it were not for the stubborn resistance of Barrell's and

Ligonier's Regiments. The battle was ultimately decided by the Jacobite reserve composed of the disciplined regulars of the Irish Picquets and the Regiment Royal Ecossais, and Hawley's army beat a hasty retreat back to Falkirk. The aftermath of the battle was recounted in grisly style by Robert Chambers, a private volunteer in Hawley's army:-

"The succeeding day, during which it continued to rain with little intermission, was spent at Falkirk by the insurgents in securing the spoils and burying the slain. They employed the country people to dig a spacious pit upon the field of battle, into which they precipitated the naked corpses. The rustics who stood around easily distinguished the English soldiers from the Highlanders by their comparative nudity, and by the deep gashes which seamed their shoulders and breasts - the dreadful work of the broadsword." [107]

The battle had lasted for only a short time, perhaps as little as forty minutes, but the government casualties were out of all proportion to the time that the armies had been engaged. They lost perhaps 280 men in killed and wounded, including a number of senior officers. Sir Robert Munro, Colonel of the 37th Foot, Lt Col Powell of Chomondley's and Colonel Whiting of Ligonier's Dragoons were all killed, and Colonel Ligonier himself, son of the General who had commanded the government forces in the midlands during the march south, died a few days later of his wounds. In addition the Jacobites took about 300 prisoners and their own casualties probably did not exceed 50 killed and 80 wounded. However, the government forces were able to retreat in relatively good order, and the battle had been much harder fought than the easy victory at Prestonpans only four months before; at last the redcoats seemed to be getting the measure of the Jacobite army.

This hard-won but well-deserved victory could have been followed up and turned into a catastrophe for the government forces in Scotland, but instead the Prince chose to return to the siege of Stirling Castle. However, by 1st February he had decided to abandon the siege, the guns were spiked and the Jacobites left their trenches. In the meantime Hawley's army had retreated unpursued to Edinburgh where, over the next two months, they were joined by three battalions of foot, two regiments of dragoons and some artillerymen under the Duke of Cumberland.

It had been the Prince's wish to renew his attack on the Duke's army, but he had received a pessimistic assessment of the state of his army from Lord George Murray, so after a somewhat acrimonious council of war, convened by the Prince notwithstanding the resolution he had expressed at Derby never to hold another one, a further retreat to the highlands, the heartland of the rebellion, was decided upon. By mid February the Prince's army was concentrated near Inverness which they captured on the 18th. After this, in a desultory campaign lacking any strategic direction, they went on to capture Fort Augustus, Fort George and Ruthven barracks and then besiege Fort William which held out and from which they were ultimately forced to retreat.

In the meantime Cumberland had not been idle, but had transferred his troops to the Jacobite stronghold of Aberdeen which he successfully occupied and which became the base of his operations against his diminished, and increasingly hungry and demoralised, opponents. In early April he began to move north and then west to meet the Prince's army. On 16th April 1746, on the bleak and windswept ground of Drumossie Moor, Culloden as it is now called, the two sides met at what was to be the last battle on British soil.

By this time the Jacobite army was much reduced, both in numbers and morale. the logistical arrangements had almost entirely broken down, and many of the highlanders were away foraging for food. When the action began, at about 1 pm, the Jacobites probably numbered no more than about 5,500 men to the Duke's 7,000. There had been an abortive march by the Jacobites the previous night carried out in the hope of taking the enemy camp by surprise while they were celebrating the Duke's birthday. However, the march was much more difficult and took much longer than had been expected, and by the time they arrived the government camp was astir and an attack was out of the question. The army had to wend its weary way back, and as a consequence many of the clansmen were exhausted before the battle even began. Cumberland's army had other advantages as well as numbers. They were well rested after a good night's sleep, the troops were well trained, their morale was high and they were led by efficient and experienced officers. In addition, most of the men present were tough battle-hardened veterans of the fighting in Flanders and the administrative arrangements had ensured that they were all well-fed and watered. Lastly, they had a good train of artillery consisting of ten 3 pounders and 6 Coehorn mortars well-served by the professionals of the Royal Regiment of Artillery. The Jacobite artillery, by contrast, always the weakest element of their army in any event, was both outnumbered by the enemy's and mainly served by volunteers who knew little of the technicalities of using artillery in the field.

When the action began the Jacobites had first to sustain a bombardment from the Cumberland's artillery to which they could make no effective reply. Becoming restless under the enemy's fire, the right wing of the Jacobite army, consisting of the Atholl Brigade, the Camerons and the Appin Regiment, without orders, charged the Duke's left wing, but were met by ferocious and well-disciplined volley fire. With extraordinary gallantry they pressed their attack and broke into the first line of the redcoats, inflicting some 120 casualties on Barrell's Regiment and more than 80 on Munro's. However, disciplined fire power told against them and of the estimated 500 clansmen who reached the front line of the Hanoverian army, virtually none escaped death or serious injury. Cumberland hastily brought up his reserves and the charge faltered to a halt.

In the meantime the left wing of the Jacobites, composed of the Clan Donald Regiments of Keppoch, Clanranald and Glengarry, had hardly taken part in the battle at all. They had embarked on the action piqued by the decision to give them the left wing rather than the place of honour on the right wing which went to the Atholl Brigade. In addition, because the Jacobite line was angled away from their opponents, the left wing was much further away from the enemy than the right wing was, and consequently they had more ground to cover, much of it boggy and difficult terrain which impeded the speed and weight of the highland charge and upon which they had so often relied for victory. To all intents and purposes it was their only tactic.

The initial charge of the left wing had hardly started before Clan Donald began to waver and turn back, leaving MacDonald of Keppoch and his son to advance alone against the redcoats. As he did so he shouted despairingly in Gaelic, "Have the sons of my clan deserted me?" and was cut down by a blast of grapeshot from the Hanoverian artillery. As the Jacobite attack started to break down, the Hanoverian left wing moved to encircle their opponent's right, and the highland army began to dissolve in bloodshed and confusion. The Prince's escape was only possible because of the steady rearguard action of the French regular troops, the Irish Picquets and the Regiment Royal Ecossais, whose commander, Brigadier Stapleton, was killed in the retreat. Chevalier Johnstone describes the battle in his usual vivid style:-

"The English were drawn up in three lines, but we had much difficulty in forming two.......When the English army was on a line with the enclosure.....our army descended with great rapidity into the marshy ground and charged the enemy sword in hand.........From the inequality of this marshy ground, our right and centre came first up with the enemy, our first line advancing a little obliquely; but, overpowered by a murderous fire in front and flank, our right could not maintain its ground and was obliged to give way, whilst our centre had already broken the enemy's first line and attacked the second. The left wing, where I was with Scothouse, was not twenty paces from the enemy, who gave their first fire at the moment the flight began to become general, which spread from the right to the left of our army with the rapidity of lightning. What a spectacle of horror! The same Highlanders who had advanced to the charge like lions, with bold, determined countenances, were in an instant seen flying like trembling cowards in the greatest disorder......As far as I could distinguish....the English seemed to be drawn up in six ranks, the three first being on their knees, and keeping up a terrible running fire upon us. My unfortunate friend Scothouse was killed by my side..." [108]

This was a decisive victory for the Duke of Cumberland's army; they lost perhaps 60 killed and 270 wounded of whom a number died later of their wounds. The Jacobites, by contrast, lost over 1,000 killed and more than 500 taken prisoner. After the battle, while the highlanders retreated to Ruthven barracks, hotly pursued by the dragoons of Kingston's Horse, few prisoners were taken, and many of the Jacobite wounded were murdered in cold blood on the battlefield.

The aftermath of the battle has been covered in detail in a number of historical accounts, notably that of John Prebble in his gripping, but not always accurate, book "Culloden". The terrible retribution meted out to the defeated Jacobites after the battle, and the subsequent harrying of the highlands by government troops, falls outside the scope of this work, but it was ruthless and bloody and carried out without regard to the suffering of the highlanders and their families, with many men, women and children being butchered and property looted and destroyed

Of the major protagonists in this extraordinary series of events, the Prince himself, after five months on the run in the highlands, fraught with danger and hair's breadth escapes, and with a price of £30,000 on his head, eventually managed to escape to France in September. He returned, secretly, to London in 1750 and was received into the Anglican Church in the faint hope that this would improve his chances of restoring the Stuart line, but he never again had an opportunity of putting his hopes to the test of war, and declined into an abusive and drink-sodden alcoholic. He died in Rome in 1788. Lord

George Murray also managed to escape to France and died in exile in Holland in 1760. His brother William, titular Duke of Atholl, was captured and died in the Tower of London. Donald Cameron of Lochiel, after being seriously wounded at Culloden, also managed to escape but his health had been permanently affected and he died in 1748. Lord Elcho, whose narrative tells us so much about the march into England and the occupation of Derby, also managed to escape to France, became an officer in the French service and survived until 1787. Lord Ogilvie, who commanded the cavalry on the retreat from Derby, lived longer than any of them, dying in 1803. James Drummond, Duke of Perth, did manage to reach the safety of a French ship but died on the voyage home. Lord Balmerino, whose cavalry carried out so many of the raids around Derby during the occupation, was unusual amongst senior Jacobite officers in failing to make good his escape to the continent. He was captured and suffered execution on Tower Green on 18th August 1746 together with Lord Kilmarnock and the Earl of Cromartie. On the government side, Cumberland was lionised as a hero and died in 1765. William Cavendish, 3rd Duke of Devonshire, whose "Derbyshire Blues" preformed so poorly during the invasion of the county, spent his declining years trying to reconcile his wife and his eldest son.

Of the minor characters in our story, Francis Townley, Colonel of the Manchester Regiment, was left with his men as part of the garrison at Carlisle and was captured with most of them when it fell to the Duke of Cumberland on 30th December 1745. He was tried for high treason, convicted and condemned to death and executed on Kennington Common on 30th July 1746. Ten of his officers suffered the same fate, including the chaplain, the Rev Thomas Coppock, who had celebrated the service at All Saints Church on 5th December. Also executed at Kennington Common on 1st November 1746 was that constant braggart James Sparkes who had been captured while foraging a few days after the retreat from Derby had begun. One wonders whether, had his support for the Prince had been a little less vociferous and public, he might have escaped the gallows and simply suffered transportation to Barbados as did so many of his fellows. As to the fate of the Derby blacksmith Humphrey Cook, the butcher Edward Hewit, and Private William Morris, all of the Manchester Regiment, the record is silent; they may well have died in captivity. One Derby man who had enlisted in the Manchester regiment, Charles Webster, was acquitted. The engaging Lancashire volunteer John Daniel made good his escape to France.

Altogether some 3,500 men and women were taken prisoner after the Rising; one third of them were transported to the colonies and

120 were executed. Of all the regiments that marched to Derby it was, predictably, the Manchester regiment that suffered the worst. Eleven of its officers, all but one of its eight sergeants, and nine of the rank and file were executed and most of the rest either died in captivity or were transported [109]. Deaths in captivity due to overcrowding, starvation and neglect were commonplace. Out of 303 prisoners transported by sea from Scotland to Tilbury on 10th June 1746, at least 46 died and it may have been many more. Those who took part in the doomed rising suffered the most severe penalties and the Hanoverian succession was never again seriously challenged. There were continued Jacobite plots, but the Jacobite Cause was effectively at an end.

The government ordered a national day of prayer and thanksgiving on 9th October 1746 for their victory at Culloden, noted by James Clegg :-

"This was the thanksgiving day for the victory over the Rebels. I preached to a pretty full congregation from Ezra 9:13, 14th and was about three hours in the pulpit and not much spent, after dinner I walked up to Chappell." [110]

In many churches up and down the land, the bells were rung in celebration of the end of the rebellion. There is no record in the church wardens' accounts of All Saints Derby of any payment to bell ringers on this occasion, but we can be reasonably sure that the bells pealed out all the same. We do know that a celebratory sermon was preached on that day in Derby by one E Latham using the text from Judges Verse 9: "My heart is toward the Governours of Israel, that offered themselves willingly among the People: Bless ye the Lord". It described the terror of the people of Derby during the invasion of the previous December due to the "frightful appearance", "dire threatenings" and "horrid oaths and curses of the Jacobites", made the usual references to "popish rage and cruelty" and noted that had they succeeded, "Adieu then Liberty and Property: Adieu to our Laws and Religion" - a neat summary of the very factors that deterred most people from joining the Prince in his doomed attempt to regain the throne for his father.

The clan system in the highlands never recovered from its defeat at Culloden. After the battle the government passed a number of Acts to prohibit the carrying of weapons by highlanders and to proscribe the wearing of tartan and the playing of the bagpipes; the speaking and writing of Gaelic was effectively outlawed. The traditional law-making and judicial functions of the clan chiefs were abolished, and the estates of the senior Jacobite leaders were confiscated and administered by the Crown. These provisions, or, at least, some of them, were only reversed in 1784. All this opened the way for the Highland Clearances of the Nineteenth century many of which, to their eternal shame, were carried out by the clan chiefs under the guise of "improving" their land. But the legacy of the rising remained in the many plangent and melancholy songs commemorating "Bliadhna Tearlaich" - the year of Prince Charles.

Chapter 12

Could the Prince have won?

Many years ago the distinguished historian of the Jacobite movement, Sir Charles Petrie, wrote a beguiling piece of counter-factual history entitled "If: A Jacobite Fantasy". In this article he imagines that the Prince overrides his commanders at the council of war at Derby, and marches on towards London. The Jacobites reach Oxford on 10th December, and at eleven o'clock that night the sentries from the Manchester Regiment on Magdalen Bridge hear a coach approaching - "the guard had hardly time to parade before there burst upon their astonished sight a coach and six driven at a breakneck gallop and escorted by a troop of dragoons in the Elector's uniform, but wearing white cockades. The equipage was halted and the cavalry disarmed, and there then descended from the coach with his wig on one side and his teeth chattering with terror His Grace the Duke of Newcastle, Prime Minister of Great Britain [sic - the Prime Minister was actually Henry Pelham]. The panic-stricken statesman was hurried to the Prince, before whom he fell on his knees ejaculating incoherently, "He's gone back to Hanover!" It is perhaps the most dramatic episode in English history." [111]

Ever since then historians, both academic and popular, have been tempted down the path of speculation to wonder whether, if a different decision had been reached at Derby, the Prince might actually have succeeded in restoring the Stuarts to the throne. Surprisingly, perhaps, many of them have concluded that a triumphant highland army entering the capital is by no means improbable, although it is equally true to say that many modern historians of the rising would disagree. Simpson, in his book "Derby and the Forty-Five," makes clear where his own sympathies lie in his glimpse into the future :-

"... by the time Charles had got as far as Northampton, the Welsh would have been on the way, either to join him, or to link up with Beaufort and, on the assumption that the Prince designed to reach Leicester in a day's march, he could have fought and won his battle, and been in London by the 11th December. The news of the debacle of Northampton would have done all that was needed, the country would have been up, Barrymore would have roused Lancashire and Cheshire more effectually than even the presence of the Prince had been able to do, and the camp at Finchley would have been found to be the hopeless gamble it really was." [112]

Petrie, in his book "The Jacobite Movement" (Third edition 1958) says:-

"In the light of all the available evidence, then, it is difficult to resist the conclusion that if Charles had marched forward from Derby he would have won the crown for his father. The opposition to the Stuarts was noisy rather than formidable, while so far as London was concerned there were a good number of influential Jacobites only waiting for the right moment to declare themselves". [113]

More recently, in his magisterial work "The '45", even Christopher Duffy seems to have succumbed to the peculiar attractions of imagining a Jacobite victory, or, at least, its possibility, concluding "Yes, Prince Charles should have advanced from Derby, for that course offered a realistic, if incalculable, chance of success, as against the near certainty of the destruction of the armed Jacobite cause." [114]

With some trepidation, therefore, particularly in the face of such erudition, I intend to take the opposite view in this book, and the reader must make his or her own judgement as to which outcome is the more likely on the basis of the evidence.

Let us first of all consider the state of the Jacobite army on 6th December 1745. We can be reasonably certain that its numbers were nowhere near the 7,500 odd men which the billeting details would indicate. This figure was arrived at by counting the numbers of men billeted in each parish during the time that the Jacobites occupied the town. However, there was almost certainly a substantial degree of double-counting, and most authorities assess the strength of the highland army at no more than about 5,500 to 6,000 men. They had probably lost about 1,000 men by desertion on the march down, and although some of these losses had been made up by the recruitment of men in Manchester, it went only a small way towards making up the difference. By the time they reached Derby they still had with them the 13 pieces of light artillery that they had brought from Scotland, including a small Coehorn mortar, but they had very few trained men to serve the guns and transporting them over the rough roads of the day had proved difficult. The morale of the army rank and file was high, deservedly so. They had achieved an astonishing march into England without any appreciable opposition and were now within 100 miles of the capital.

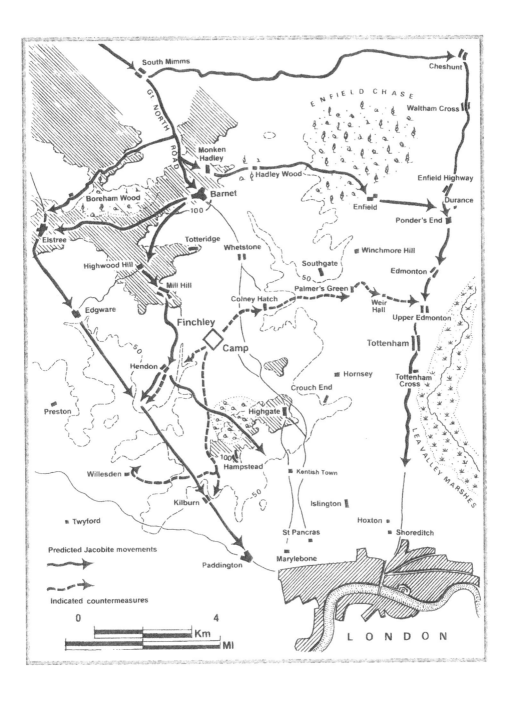

5. The Contest for London; presumed Jacobite thrusts and planned counter-measures

There can be little doubt that the clan regiments, in particular, were euphoric at the prospect that London, and hence the country as a whole, would soon be theirs. The Jacobite leadership, however, was a totally different matter. From the outset there had been tensions between the "old guard" who had accompanied the Prince to Scotland, especially his Irish advisers Sir Thomas Sheridan and John William O'Sullivan on the one hand, and the senior Scots Jacobite commanders, in particular Lord George Murray and David Lord Elcho, on the other. Murray had never been wholly enthusiastic about the invasion, but had consented to go along with it on the understanding that the position would be reviewed if no substantial numbers of English recruits appeared. The army had now marched more than 200 miles into England and had managed to recruit a pathetic 300 or so (at most), many of them unemployed cloth workers from Manchester and other parts of Lancashire without military experience or training. These tensions became very apparent during the council of war on 5th December, and it became clear that the only person who wished to press on with the march regardless was the Prince himself.

However, there is one intriguing aspect of local Jacobite support raised by Eardley-Simpson in "Derby and the Forty-Five" and pursued by other historians since. He suggests that while the Prince's army was occupying Derby, preparations were afoot in Wales for a strong force of Jacobites to join them under the leadership of a prominent Welsh Jacobite, Sir Watkin Williams Wynn. Is there any truth in this, and what difference might it have made to the decision of the council of war? This possibility seems to have arisen because of a letter written by the Prince to his father from Avignon in February 1747. In it he states that a Mr Barry, a son of another long-time Jacobite, the Earl of Barrymore who was based at Marbury in Cheshire, "arrived at Derby two days after I parted. He had been sent by Sir Watkin Wynn and Lord Barrymore to assure me, that they were ready to join me in what manner I pleased, either in the capital, or every one to rise in his own country". Wynn and Barrymore had previously worked closely in conjunction with each other, and it is certainly true that the Prince wrote to Barrymore from Brampton near Carlisle on 11th November:-

"My Lord,
This is to acquaint you with the success we have had since our arrival in Scotland, and how far we are advanced without repulse. We are now a numerous army, and are laying siege to Carlisle this day, which we are sure cannot hold out long. After that we intend to take our

route straight for London, and if things answer our expectations we design to be in Cheshire before the 24th inst. Then I hope you and all my friends in that county will be ready to join us. For now is the time or never. Adieu.

Charles, Prince Regent." [115]

Unfortunately for Charles, the letter was delivered, in Barrymore's absence, to his Whig and Hanoverian supporting son Lord Buttevant who immediately burned it. There is no direct evidence that Charles tried to contact Wynn in a similar fashion. At the time Wynn was attending Parliament in London and trying to keep his head down having drawn upon himself the suspicion of the government the previous year; he was not, as has been asserted by Eardley-Simpson and others, in North Wales organising support for the Prince's invasion. Eardley-Simpson states that there was a body of Welsh Jacobites, some 300 in number, under Wynn waiting to march and join the highland army in Derby. He suggests that if they had managed a conjunction of forces, then that might have been enough to persuade the Jacobite leaders to continue their march to London. How realistic is this? Let us suppose that there really were 300 Welsh Jacobites awaiting the signal to march to Derby. They would have had to march all the way from Wrexham (where Wynn was based at Wynnstay Hall near Ruabon), through largely hostile territory in the face of large and well-organised government forces, without any logistical support. We may safely assume that few, if any, of those Jacobite supporters had had previous military experience. Like the men who joined Charles at Preston and Garstang they were essentially members of the minor gentry and their followers who, at best, would have brought their personal arms with them, but would not have constituted an army in any sense of the word. Even if they had managed to evade the government troops in Staffordshire, it is wholly improbable that this very modest accretion of strength to the Prince's army would have persuaded his hard-headed and disillusioned officers to alter their view about the viability of a continued march on London. We can, I think, dismiss this whole story as another bit of Jacobite wishful-thinking.

What of the government forces? There were basically three armies available to oppose the march on London; Field Marshal Wade's, originally based in Newcastle; this was marching south in parallel with the Jacobite army, and by 6th December was in the process of taking up quarters around Doncaster. It totalled some 12,600 troops of which 4,200 were the unreliable Swiss and Dutch, but there were also 5,000 good quality British infantry, most of whom were battle-hardened veterans of the fighting in Flanders; they included many of the regiments that were to defeat the highland army at Culloden just four months later. There were also about 1,500 cavalry and dragoons and a train of artillery manned by the professionals of the Royal Regiment of Artillery. In the Midlands the government forces were under the command of Cumberland, who was also the overall commander of all the government troops in Britain. On 2nd December he had at his command 12 battalions of regular infantry (perhaps 6,000 men) and 6 regiments, or part regiments, of cavalry and dragoons numbering about 1,200 men. These troops were quartered at various towns between Chester and Lichfield with strong forces at Newcastle-under-Lyme, Stafford and Stone, where the train of artillery was. Lastly, there was the army forming in London and intended to be deployed on Finchley Common to the north of the capital where it would be available to meet any Jacobite movement either to the east of the capital via Cheshunt, Waltham and Edmonton, or to the west via Elstree and Edgware. This included 8 battalions of regular infantry including 17 Grenadier companies of the Foot Guards, albeit some of them were new recruits, and about 500 cavalry and dragoons. In addition, there was a very powerful train of artillery in preparation at the Tower of London which was intended to march for Finchley on 9th December. This consisted of 34 field guns which could be used on the battlefield firing 3 and 4 lbs weight of shot and also, of course, able to fire the deadly anti-personnel charge known as canister or grape-shot which was to wreak such havoc amongst the highlanders at Culloden the following year.

A number of routes would have been open to the Jacobite army had they pressed on from Derby. The obvious one was the direct route south towards Loughborough and Leicester via the vital bridge at Swarkestone which had been seized by the Jacobite vanguard on 4th December. It was suggested at the time, however, by the Duke of Cumberland himself, that this might have been difficult as the roads south had been broken up and obstructed; instead he considered that the army might well have chosen to march east across the Pennines to Sheffield and hence down the Great North Road. Recent historians appear to have accepted this analysis without comment. But consider this; if the Jacobite army had chosen that route instead of the superficially more direct road south, then that would have had two vital consequences: firstly the route to Sheffield would have brought them to within 12 miles of Wade's powerful army at Doncaster. They cannot have arrived in Sheffield in under two days at best (Wade himself had found the Pennine passes further north well-nigh impassable only two weeks earlier), by which time the whole of Wade's army would have arrived at Doncaster and would have been in a position to attack the highland army with superior numbers, and with Cumberland moving up in the rear of the Prince's army to cut off both its march to London and its retreat to Scotland as they so nearly did at Clifton on 18th December. Secondly, it is debatable whether the Jacobites would have managed to cross the Pennines in the way suggested, at least with their artillery and baggage, and even if they had done so they would have arrived at their billets exhausted by the effort and in no condition to meet a relatively fresh and numerically superior opponent.

The other route was the direct route south, the one which Cumberland considered too difficult for the Jacobites; what if they had chosen that one? Most modern historians seem to think that if they had done so they would have stolen a march on both of their opponents and would have reached the vital half-way stage of Northampton before either Wade or Cumberland was able to cut them off, avoided battle, and marched on unopposed to London. This is a moot point. The marching orders for Cumberland's forces in the West Midlands indicate that no less than five regiments of Dragoons would have reached Northampton by 7th December, and they would quickly have been followed the next day by two battalions of infantry and the artillery train. By the 9th December a further seven battalions of infantry would have been deployed. It is difficult to believe that the Jacobite army, encumbered with its artillery, baggage, women and camp followers, of which there were quite a number including the wives of some of the senior Jacobite commanders, and forced to travel over roads that had been broken up and obstructed, could have reached Northampton in under three or four days. The distance between Derby and Northampton, even as the crow flies, is 52 miles, much longer by the inadequate roads of the day, perhaps as much as 75 miles over highways obstructed by felled trees; the Prince's army would have struggled to convey their artillery through the heavy snow, as witness the difficulties that they encountered only two weeks later in Cumberland. In my estimation the Jacobites would, at best, have faced a very strong force of government troops which might very well have been enough seriously to delay their march to London and to inflict significant casualties on them.

Even if, by a miracle, they had managed to avoid a clash with the government forces on their way to London, by the time they arrived there (and I do not think that they could possibly have done so before 12th December), they would have been faced with a strong force encamped at Finchley Common and two armies, each of which outnumbered their own, coming up fast in their rear. However, let us give them the benefit of every possible doubt. Let us suppose that they somehow beat the army on Finchley Common and then beat both Wade and Cumberland. What is likely to have happened when they marched into London? What was the mood in the capital city and would it have been for or against them?

There is no doubt that when news reached London of the arrival of the Prince's army in Derby, there was a degree of anxiety, sometimes verging on panic. We know this from the writings of the arch-Whig Henry Fielding author of "The History of Tom Jones", published some four years later. In September there had been a run on the Bank of England, and it is undoubtedly the fact that some city merchants were making prudent plans to flee. However, the King was not, as has been alleged, simply waiting for a signal to board his yacht in the Thames and sail to the continent. On the contrary he was waiting to join his army at Finchley and lead it from the front as he had done at the Battle of Dettingen only some two years before. There is absolutely no evidence to support the assertion that the Secretary of State, the Duke of Newcastle, spent the day locked in his rooms deciding whether or not to go over to the other side. In any event, even if the King and government had taken prudent steps to save themselves, that does not necessarily mean to say that the whole government would have collapsed the minute the first kilted highlander reached the city. In 1940, when invasion from Germany was a much more realistic threat, Winston Churchill had made plans to evacuate himself and the Royal Family to Canada where the struggle would have been continued. There is no doubt that the government of the country was solidly Whig, whatever the secret sympathies of some of the people might have been. The Whig party completely dominated the government of Britain from 1715 until 1760 - even the Tory government of Lord North in 1770 was composed mainly of former Whigs who had defected! To suppose, therefore, that the government in London would simply have capitulated or changed sides if the Prince had entered the capital is to prefer romantic imagination to the realities of power politics - the simple truth is that there were too many powerful people with too much invested in the Hanoverian succession to make the overthrow of the government possible, still less likely. As for the attitude of the middle class in London, the traders, bankers and merchants, whatever their sentimental attachment to the Stuarts might have been, their commercial interests had led them to favour the Hanoverians ever since the accession of George I thirty-one years before. It is well nigh unthinkable that they would have turned to an unknown Stuart prince in preference to the German dynasty under which they had risen to prosperity. Trade and commerce had made England great over the first half of the 18th Century, and no-one was about to give that up in a hurry.

The threat that caused the greatest anxiety to the government in December 1745 was not just the approaching Jacobite army, but the distinct possibility of a French invasion of the south coast. They could handle one but not both. Sir Horace Walpole, historian, man of letters and son of the Whig politican Sir Robert Walpole, writing to Sir Horace Mann on 9th December makes this clear and also comments on the failure of the Jacobites to raise any support on their march south and the prevailing support for the government in the capital:-

"We are threatened with great preparations for a French invasion, but the coast is exceedingly guarded; and for the people, the spirit against the rebels increases every day: though they have marched thus into the heart of the kingdom, there has not been the least symptom of a rising, not even in the great towns of which they possessed themselves. They have got no recruits since their first entry into England, except one gentleman in Lancashire, one hundred and fifty common men, and two parsons, at Manchester, and a physician from York. But here in London the aversion to them is amazing: on some thoughts of the King's going to Finchley, the weavers not only offered him a thousand men, but the whole body of the Law formed themselves into a little army under the command of the Lord Chief Justice Willes, and were to have done duty at St James's, to guard the royal family in the King's absence." [116]

The French had been planning an invasion of England since 1743. They had, indeed, assembled troops and an invasion fleet in early 1744, but this was dispersed by a fierce storm on 24th February. After that, French enthusiasm for a descent on England waned. However, the Prince's victory at Prestonpans, and his subsequent, seemingly unopposed, march into England in November revived French hopes that they could deal a stunning blow to the enemy by invading his heartland in combination with the Jacobite rebels. Accordingly, from October onwards, fresh plans were made and by December the French had an invasion force of about 15,000 men gathered at Dunkirk under the command of the Duc de Richelieu. The plan was to sail the fleet down the coast to Boulogne and to launch the invasion from there. There were, in addition, 1,000 horses for the cavalry and some thirty transport barges to ship them across the Channel, accompanied by a frigate and several gunboats. To oppose this force, the commander in the Channel, Admiral Vernon, had two fifty gun men of war, two of forty guns and twenty or so smaller vessels including privateers. On 25th December some of the privateers managed to sink a number of the French transport ships. There is little doubt that this setback adversely affected the attitude of the French government to the invasion plan. The Duc de Richelieu had arrived to take command on 17th December, but was concerned that there was insufficient artillery and that more transports were needed. On the day after he learned that the Jacobites had retreated from Derby, so one important prop in the whole plan had been kicked away. In addition, the attitude of King Louis XV, and, more importantly, of his very experienced and able commander Maurice de Saxe, premier soldier of Europe, was ambivalent to say the least. During the rest of December Vernon was able to deploy his ships in the Channel, he had previously been unable to do so owing to contrary winds, and by the end of January any realistic prospect of an invasion had evaporated.

Could the French have landed, and if so, could that have tipped the balance in the Prince's favour? It is clear that French preparations would not have allowed any invasion to take place until late December at the earliest, probably the worst time of year to mount a seaborne invasion across the Channel. Even if they had managed to set sail from Dunkirk or Boulogne, it is likely that adverse weather would have made the crossing extremely difficult even without the intervention of the Royal Navy. If Vernon had managed to deploy even two of his men of war, they would have played havoc with the unarmed open decked invasion barges. Even if the French had managed to land the bulk of their (no doubt seasick) men, horses and artillery on the south coast, their chances of mounting a successful assault on the capital would have been slight and, in the unlikely event of their actually establishing themselves in London, is it seriously suggested that they would have been welcomed by the population of the country with which they had been at war, on and off, for the past fifty years and longer? It is difficult to conceive of even the presence of a sizeable French (and Catholic) force succeeding in reconciling the English to a Stuart monarch; on the contrary, a French invasion of England would have united the population behind the Hanoverian dynasty as nothing else could have done. Attempted invasions in support of the Jacobites had been planned or attempted in 1708, 1719 and 1743, all had failed, and there is no reason to think that the planned invasion of 1744 would have had a different outcome. That does not mean to say that the government was unconcerned about the threat of invasion; on the contrary, it caused them intense anxiety throughout December and early January. However, their fears were exaggerated, and the retreat of the Prince's army removed the possibility of an attack on two fronts at once. If, by a miracle, the French had managed to land in mid-December, then troops would have been available to rush south to defend the approaches to London.

What of the infamous London Mob? Historians sympathetic to the Jacobite cause suggest that the London Mob was only waiting to declare itself for the Stuarts and that this would have been the deciding factor. This is highly arguable. There is no doubt that observers at the time considered that the Jacobite cause was especially attractive to those on the margins of society. "The Mob", smugglers and highwaymen are all referred to as likely to have Jacobite sympathies. We can safely exclude highwaymen as having any influence at all on the outcome. Smuggling was certainly rife in many coastal areas, particularly in the south and south west. There is no doubt that certain smuggling gangs had connections with the Jacobite exiles and occasionally helped to smuggle agents and money into England, but we can safely assume that this was, in the main, a purely commercial transaction. In any event, one can hardly imagine that even a gang as powerful as the Hawkhurst Gang in Kent would have had any real weight to add to the Jacobite military effort. The London Mob was a different matter. It was a considerable influence on political affairs in the capital throughout the 18th century, but was never in a position to topple governments - at best it could cause disruption, sometimes on a large scale, but it is doubtful if this would have materially assisted the Jacobite cause even if it had come out on its side. It is probable, however, that whatever the sympathies of the Mob were perceived to be, it would have hesitated before casting in its lot with the Prince. If there was one constant in the attitude of the London Mob it was its virulent anti-Catholicism. Only 15 years later it was taking over the streets on behalf of the anti-Scottish arch-Whig John Wilkes, of "Wilkes and Liberty" fame, and in 1780 London experienced the worst riots in its history when a mob, whipped into a frenzy by Lord George Gordon over the issue of the proposed Catholic Relief Act, took over the capital for several days, set fire to many buildings, razed Newgate Prison to the ground and themselves suffered several hundred fatal casualties. Even then, it was the rioters that suffered most and they were subdued with relative ease by the army. Is it seriously suggested, therefore, that the London Mob would come out in support of a Catholic Prince, the scion of a Catholic dynasty which had been deposed because its

Catholicism made it deeply unacceptable to the British people? This seems wholly improbable.

The one factor that might have assisted the Jacobites, had they been fortunate enough to reach London unscathed, was the attitude of the government troops at Finchley. Would any significant portion of them have mutinied in support of the Prince? This is a difficult question to answer. It was certainly the case that there were two Scots regiments among the troops gathering outside London, Murrays 43rd Foot (the Black Watch) and the 1st battalion of St Clair's 1st Foot (the Royal Scots). There is some suggestion that there was a degree of dissatisfaction within the ranks of both regiments, to put it no higher. At Pontefract in October one private in the Royal Scots had been given 1,000 lashes for drinking the health of James III, and the loyalty of the Black Watch is said to have been in doubt. It is not clear why this was thought to be the case. The Black Watch was composed of Whig clansmen such as the Munros and Campbells who had long supported the Hanoverian succession and it is difficult to imagine that they would have gone over to their traditional clan enemies en masse. Even if they had, it must be doubtful whether that alone would have been enough to tip the balance in the Prince's favour. In any event, dissatisfaction or not, the fact remains that, after the battle of Prestonpans, the regulars of the British army fought the Jacobites effectively and with vigour wherever they encountered them.

To summarise then, a small depleted Jacobite army, numbering no more than 6,000 men in the middle of England more than 300 miles away from its heartland in Scotland would have stood no chance against three separate Hanoverian armies outnumbering it by more than three to one. The chances of a successful French invasion in their support were negligible. Even if, by a miracle, they had managed to enter the capital, there is no way that they could have held a city of 500,000 people by themselves. There was little prospect of any substantial support from the populace as evidenced by the fact that in their march into England the Prince had managed to attract only pathetically few recruits. The 300 men of the Manchester Regiment, untrained and unmotivated except by poverty, would have melted away at the first whiff of grapeshot. It was a noble effort, which had succeeded beyond the Prince's wildest expectations, but the decision to retreat at Derby was the only sensible one to make. Whatever decision had been reached at the council of war, the rising was doomed, and had probably been doomed from the very first moment that the Prince Charles Edward set foot upon the Isle of Eriskay. The only surprising thing is that the rebels performed as well as they did. They could not have won in the long run. The spirit of the times was against them. [117]

FINIS

Chronology

1625 – King Charles I accedes to the throne

1649 – King Charles is executed

1650 – Oliver Cromwell beats the Scots at Dunbar

1651 – 1654 – Cromwell conquers Scotland

1660 – King Charles II accedes to the throne

1685 – King James II accedes to the throne (Charles II's brother)

1688 – "The Glorious Revolution" – James is deposed and William of Orange succeeds him

1689 – The Jacobite War – victory of Killiecrankie by "Bonnie Dundee"

1692 – The Massacre of Glencoe – Jacobite MacDonalds massacred by pro-government Campbells

1707 – The Act of Union. Scottish Parliament abolished. Scotland united with England under one parliament

1708 – First Jacobite Rebellion

1714 – Queen Anne dies without heirs & is succeeded by the Elector of Hanover (George I)

1715 – Second Jacobite Rebellion – Battles of Preston & Sherrifmuir

1719 – Third Jacobite Rebellion – Battle of Glenshiel & attack on Eilean Donan Castle

1720 – Prince Charles Edward Stuart born (the Young Pretender)

1720-1740 – Pacification of Highlands under General Wade – building of "Wade's Roads"

1741 – War of the Austrian Succession begins with France

1744 – Prince Charles travels to Dunkirk to accompany French on abortive invasion of England

1745 – 5th July –Charles sails from France with seven followers (the "Seven Men of Moidart")

   " - 23rd July – Charles lands on Eriskay

   " - 25th July – Charles lands on the mainland at Loch nan Uamh

   " - 19th August – Charles raises his standard at Glenfinnan

   " - 27th August – Rendezvous of Jacobite clansmen at Aberchalder

   " - 3rd September – Jacobite army captures Perth

   " - 17th September – Jacobites capture Edinburgh (but not the castle)

   " - 21st September – Battle of Prestonpans – Jacobite victory over General Cope

   " - 9th to 19th October – French ships land £5,000 in gold, 2,500 muskets & artillery at Montrose

" - 1st November – Jacobite army leaves Edinburgh for invasion of England

" - 8th November – Jacobites cross the River Esk into England

" - 10th to 15th November – Carlisle Castle besieged & captured

" - 26th November - Jacobites reach Preston

" - 29th November – Jacobites reach Manchester

" - 2nd December - Jacobites reach Leek

" - 3rd December - Jacobites reach Ashbourne

" - 4th December – Jacobites reach Derby

" - 5th December - Jacobites occupy Derby; Kedleston Hall raided for arms. Council of War decides on retreat to Scotland

" - 6th December – Jacobite army begins retreat from Derby; Prince Charles stays the night at Ashbourne Hall

" - 9th December - Jacobite army reaches Manchester

" -18th December – Action at Clifton in Cumberland

" - 20th December – Jacobites re-cross the Scottish border

" - 25th December – Jacobites reach Glasgow

" - 30th December – Carlisle garrison surrenders to Hanoverian army

1746 – 4th January – Prince's army unites with troops under Lord John Drummond

" - 17th January – Battle of Falkirk – Jacobite army beats General Hawley & his troops

" - 18th January to 1st February – Unsuccessful siege of Stirling Castle by Jacobites

" - 30th January – Duke of Cumberland re-captures Edinburgh

" - 1st February - Jacobites retreat to the Highlands

" - 19th February – Jacobite army concentrates near Inverness

" - 20th March to 3rd April – Unsuccessful siege of Fort William by Jacobites

" - 16th April – Battle of Culloden – Jacobite army defeated by Duke of Cumberland – Charles flees

" - April to December – the harrying of the Highlands – punitive expeditions sent into Jacobite areas - many men killed, women raped and property burned and stolen

" - 19th September – after many months as a fugitive Charles escapes from Loch nan Uamh to France

1746-1748 – Various Disarming Acts outlaw possession of weapons & wearing of highland dress

1746 -1748 – Many Jacobite prisoners are executed or transported to Barbados & America

1748 – Treaty of Aix La Chapelle ends the War of the Austrian Succession – end of French support

1750 – Charles makes secret visit to London & converts to Anglican Church

1752 – Jacobites hatch plot to murder George III and kidnap his family ("the Elibank Plot")

1753 – Dr Archibald Cameron of Lochiel (brother of "gentle Lochiel") executed for his part in the Elibank Plot – the last Jacobite to be executed for treason

1766 - Death of James III & accession of Bonnie Prince Charlie to the throne as Charles III

1788 – Death of Bonnie Prince Charlie in Rome

Appendix 1

Dramatis Personae

HANOVERIANS

King George II (1683-1760) - George Augustus, Elector of Hanover (always referred to as "the Elector" by Jacobites). Acceded to the throne in 1727. Absent in Hanover at the outbreak of the rising but returned to London in August 1745. A courageous and determined man, the last British monarch to lead his troops into battle personally at the Battle of Dettingen in 1743

Cavendish, William, 3rd Duke of Devonshire (1698 - 1755) - Grandson of the 1st Duke who engineered the deposition of King James II and the most prominent Whig in Derbyshire. At the time of the rising he was the Lord Lieutenant of the county and was responsible for raising the "Derbyshire Blues" regiment. A faithful and loving husband (unusually for a Cavendish), an honest but rather dilatory administrator and politician. Had previously been Lord Lieutenant of Ireland.

Cumberland, William Augustus, Duke of (1721 - 65) - A younger son of George II, usually referred to as "stinking Billy" or "the Butcher" by Jacobites and as "sweet William" by Hanoverian supporters (the flower is named after him). Commander in chief of the government forces from late 1745 and the victor of the Battle of Culloden. Responsible for much of the repression in the highlands after the rising was crushed (hence his Jacobite appellation). Received the thanks of Parliament and a grant of £25,000 for his services. Was at Stafford with part of his forces when the Jacobites marched into Derby and pursued them relentlessly on their retreat.

Wade, Field Marshal George (1673 - 1748) - The elderly and infirm commander of the government forces based in Newcastle who failed to intercept the Jacobite army as it marched south from Carlisle.

JACOBITES

Prince Charles Edward Stuart (1720 - 1788) - "The Young Pretender" and elder son to King James III ("the Old Pretender" to Hanoverians) and the hero of our story. Escaped to France in September 1746 after five months on the run in the highlands. Later in life degenerated into an abusive womaniser and alcoholic

Atholl, William Murray Duke of (1689 - 1746) - an elder brother of Lord George Murray and titular Duke of Atholl in the Jacobite peerage, also known as the Marquis of Tullibardine. Out in the risings of 1715 and 1719 and attainted. Accompanied Price Charles to Scotland as one of the "seven men of Moidart". Captured after Culloden and died in the Tower of London

Balmerino, Arthur Elphinstone, 6th Baron (1688 - 1746) - Out in the rising of 1715. Marched with the Prince to Derby in the '45 as commander of the second troop of the Prince's lifeguards. Surrendered after Culloden and was executed on Tower Hill in 1746 with Kilmarnock

Cameron, Donald of Lochiel (1695 - 1748) - "The Gentle Lochiel". Succeeded to the chieftainship of Clan Cameron in 1719. One of Charles' earliest and most dedicated adherents and marched with the Prince to Derby as commander of the Clan Cameron regiment. Wounded at Falkirk and Culloden and escaped to France where he took service with the French army. Was present at the Council of War on 5th December 1745

Drummond, James, 3rd Duke of Perth (1713 - 46) - Lieutenant General of the Jacobite army jointly with Lord George Murray. Present at the Council of War. Escaped after Culloden but died on the way back to France

Elcho, David Wemyss Lord (1721 - 87) - Joined Charles at Edinburgh in September 1745 and served throughout the rising as commander of the Prince's Lifeguard. Also present at the Council of War where he spoke strongly against a further advance to London. Escaped to France and wrote a lengthy account of the rising which is now one of the most important primary sources.

Forbes, Alexander, 4th Lord Pitsligo (1678 - 1762) - Lifelong Jacobite, out in the rising of 1715. Commanded a regiment of cavalry on the march to Derby and which formed the rearguard on 6th December 1745. Escaped after Culloden and continued to live in hiding on his estates protected and concealed by his clansmen. One of the oldest Jacobite commanders of the campaign.

Kilmarnock, William Boyd 4th Earl of (1704 - 1746). Marched with Charles to Derby as commander of a troop of horse. Captured after Culloden and executed with Balmerino

MacDonald, Alexander of Keppoch (c1693 - 1746) - Marched with Charles to Derby as commander of the clan regiment. Present at the Council of War. Killed at Culloden

Murray, Lord George (c1700 - 1760) - Son of 1st Duke of Atholl and brother of James 2nd Duke and Hanoverian supporter, and of William Murray Duke of Atholl (see above). Joined Prince Charles at Perth and was effectively the commander of the Jacobite army throughout the campaign. Was present at the Council of War at Derby where he urged retreat. Escaped to France after Culloden

Murray, John of Broughton (1715 - 77) - Jacobite agent and secretary to Prince Charles. Asked for his opinion at the Council of War when he inadvertently entered the room where it was being held at Exeter House. After the rising turned King's evidence and was pardoned in 1748. Execrated as a traitor by Jacobite supporters

Ogilvy, David, Earl of Airlie (1725 - 1803) - Marched to Derby, accompanied by his "very beautiful" wife. Commanded the Jacobite cavalry on the retreat. Fought at Falkirk and Culloden. Escaped to France and restored to full rights in 1782

O'Sullivan, John William (1700 - c1761) - Irish professional soldier in the service of France and came over with Prince Charles. Adjutant General of the Jacobite army. Present at the Council of War. Had a tempestuous relationship with Lord George Murray whom he actively disliked. Escaped after Culloden and married a wealthy heiress. Wrote a lengthy and somewhat underrated account of the rising.

Townley (or Towneley), Francis (1709 - 1746) - Lancashire Roman Catholic gentleman and member of a staunchly Jacobite family. Joined Prince Charles at Preston and commanded the Manchester Regiment on the march to Derby. Captured at Carlisle in December 1745 and executed the following year.

APPENDIX 2
Regiments of the Jacobite Army which took part in the invasion of England

CAVALRY

Bagot's Hussars – Raised in Edinburgh in October 1745 by the Prince's Secretary, John Murray of Broughton. Commanded first by George Hamilton of Redhouse and latterly by John Bagot of the French Regiment Rooth (not Matthew Bagot as is sometimes stated). Wore a distinctive uniform of tartan waistcoat and fur trimmed hats with a red plume. Always a small unit of no more than 80 men, they were routed at Clifton in December 1745 but fought well at Culloden where their commander was wounded and captured. These were probably the troops that raided Kedleston Hall on 5th December

Lord Kilmarnock's Horseguards – Raised after Prestonpans by William Boyd, 4th Earl of Kilmarnock. Returned from the invasion in good order. In March 1746 comprised some 50 men. Handed their horses to Fitzjames's Horse and fought at Culloden as Footguards deployed near the Prince's standard. Their commander was subsequently captured and executed on Tower Hill with his compatriot Lord Balmerino.

Lord Pitsligo's Horse – Raised in Aberdeenshire by Alexander Forbes, 4th Lord Forbes of Pitsligo and numbering perhaps 130 men. Dressed in Highland clothes of some description. They were present at the siege of Carlisle and were the first unit of the Jacobite army to enter Manchester. Brought up the rear on the retreat from Derby. Fought at Culloden as Footguards with Kilmarnock's Horse

Prince's Lifeguard – Raised after Prestonpans and uniformed with blue coats faced with red, buff trousers, a belt faced with tartan, cavalry boots and a black tricorn hat. May have numbered 160 men initially, but had dwindled to 46 at Culloden. Comprised two troops, Lord Elcho's and Lord Balmerino's. The volunteers John Daniel and Robert Strange were both in Balmerino's troop.

INFANTRY

Atholl Brigade – As the name implies, this was a Brigade rather than a Regiment and was one of the strongest units in the Jacobite Army, although much troubled by desertion. Raised early in the campaign in Perthshire amongst the Murrays, Robertsons and Menzies, it consisted of three battalions nominally commanded by Lord George Murray (in fact by his second in command Robert Mercer), Lord Nairne and Menzies of Shian. It played a prominent role in the invasion. Subsequently fought at Prestonpans, Falkirk and Culloden, it probably numbered no more than 900 at its full strength; it fielded 500 men at Culloden

Cameron of Lochiel's Regiment – Raised amongst his clansmen in and around the southern end of the Great Glen and commanded by Donald Cameron of Lochiel ("the gentle Lochiel") it was one of the first regiments to be raised for the Prince and was one of the strongest numbering 500 at Prestonpans and some 700 at Culloden. Like all the clan regiments the men wore "highland cloathes" i.e. tartan belted plaid or trews (often trews for the officers to facilitate riding on horseback).

Edinburgh Regiment – As its name implies, this was a Lowland Regiment raised by John Roy Stewart in Edinburgh after its capture, and included a number of deserters from the Hanoverian army. It missed Falkirk, being engaged in the siege of Stirling, but was present at Culloden. Probably numbered around 200 men during the invasion of England.

Gordon of Glenbucket's Regiment – Raised by the septuagenarian John Gordon in Strathavon, Strathbogie and other parts of the Gordon estates. Took part in the march to Derby, but was absent at the siege of Stirling when the Battle of Falkirk took place. Probably numbered some 400 at this time. The regiment fought in the second line at Culloden.

Grant of Glenmoriston's Regiment – A small unit of perhaps 80 to 100 men raised in Glenmoriston and Glen Urquhart and commanded by Patrick Grant of Glenmoriston. Fought at Prestonpans, Falkirk and Culloden where 30 men were killed and the remaining 87 who surrendered were nearly all transported. During the march to Derby it formed part of MacDonnell of Glengarry's Regiment (see infra)

MacDonald of Clanranald's Regiment – One of the very first regiments raised and present at Glenfinnan. Fought at Prestonpans (200 strong), Falkirk (300 strong) and Culloden (200 strong). Commanded by Col Ranald MacDonald of Clanranald the Younger who was wounded at the battle.

MacDonald of Glencoe's Regiment – A small unit of no more than about 120 men raised and commanded by Alexander MacDonald of Glencoe & after Prestonpans merged with Keppoch's Regiment. It included many members of the proscribed clan of MacGregors. The regiment served throughout the campaign & surrendered on 12th May 1745.

MacDonald of Keppoch's Regiment – Raised and commanded by Alexander MacDonald of Keppoch. Joined the Prince at Glenfinnan and fought at Prestonpans, Falkirk & Culloden where Keppoch was killed heroically charging the Hanoverian infantry. Never more than about 200 strong it was the least well disciplined of the Clan Regiments.

MacDonnell of Glengarry's Regiment – A strong regiment which joined the Prince at Aberchalder. Commanded by Angus Og MacDonnell the Younger until he was shot dead accidentally at Falkirk. Then commanded by Donald MacDonnell of Lochgarry, formerly an officer in the 64th Highlanders. Fought at Prestonpans, Falkirk & Culloden, where it was about 500 strong. Heavily engaged at the skirmish at Clifton on the retreat from Derby. MacDonnell escaped to France with the Prince.

Mackinnon's Regiment – About 80 strong, raised and commanded by John MacKinnon of MacKinnon on Skye. Attached to Keppoch's Regiment. Fought at Falkirk and at the skirmish at Clifton. Missed Culloden. One of the last Jacobite regiments to disband.

MacLachlans and MacLeans Regiment – Joined the Jacobites at the outset and was attached to Nairne's Regiment in the Atholl Brigade. Commanded by the clan chief Lachlan MacLachlan of Castle Lachlan and by John MacLean of Kingairloch. Fought at Prestonpans and Falkirk and, for the first time as an independent unit, at Culloden (200 strong) where Lachlan was killed. This is the regiment in which the diarist John MacLean served on the march to Derby - he was killed at Culloden.

MacPherson of Cluny's Regiment – Raised and commanded by Ewan MacPherson of Cluny, another former officer in Loudon's 64th Highlanders who was captured with his men and joined the Prince. Not present at Prestonpans, but was with the Jacobite army in the march to Derby and fought at Falkirk (400 strong). Missed Culloden as the regiment was guarding lines of communication.

Manchester Regiment – As their names implies, recruited in Manchester in November 1745 on the march to Derby. The only regiment raised in England. Wore Blue coats with a tartan sash. Commanded by Colonel Francis Townley, an English Jacobite formerly in the French service. Up to 300 strong falling to 118 all of whom were captured at Carlisle where they were left as the garrison on the retreat to Scotland. Townley and most of his officers and NCO's were executed, probably the highest death toll of any regiment in the Jacobite army.

Lord Ogilvy's Regiment – Raised by David Lord Ogilvy (heir to the Earl of Airlie) in Angus. Initially 200 strong but supplemented later by further levies. Joined the Prince after Prestonpans and fought at Falkirk (900 strong) and Culloden (500 strong). One of the largest & best disciplined regiments in the Jacobite army and retired intact from Culloden. Their muster book is a useful source of information on the march to Derby.

Duke of Perth's Regiment – Raised and commanded by James Drummond Duke of Perth in September 1745. Strength varied between 200 and 400 men. At Prestonpans and Culloden, but not Falkirk as it was engaged in the siege of Stirling. Included highlanders, lowlanders, English volunteers & redcoat deserters.

Stewarts of Appin Regiment – Joined the Prince at Invergarry in August 1745 and served throughout the campaign. Raised and commanded by Charles Stewart of Ardshiel. Fought at Prestonpans, Falkirk & Culloden (250 strong) where it lost 90 killed and 65 wounded, one of the highest totals of any of the clan regiments

ARTILLERY

13 small pieces and a Coehorn mortar (now to be found at Kedleston Hall) commanded by Colonel James Grant, a regular in French service with Lally's Regiment.

Appendix 3

The Chronicle of the Derbyshire Regiment
With the Mighty Acts of Devonshire their Colonel
and L W their Captain

by Nathan Ben Shaddai, a Priest of the Jews

(This contemporary "squib" or satire on the performance of the Derbyshire Blues Regiment, cast in the manner of the Old Testament, is a humorous take on what happened when the braggadocio of the government supporters in Derby was confronted by the realities of the Jacobite Army's invasion)

1. And whilst these things were doing, Devonshire arose and said unto the King, O King, live for ever! Let thy Throne be established in Righteousness, and let thine Enemies fall down before the Face of thy mighty Men.

2. Behold, now if I have found Favour in thy Sight grant unto thy servant thy Royal Commission, that I may raise for thee a Regiment in the Province where I dwell; for why should thy Servant be idle when the Enemies of the King are conspiring against him

3. And the Saying pleased the King, and he answer'd and said unto him, thou hast our Leave, do as thou hast said; and of the Regiment to be raised be thou Colonel. So Devonshire took Leave and departed

4. Now this Devonshire was a Mighty Man, honour'd of his King, and belov'd of his Country; He had been Viceroy of the Kingdom of Ireland, and moreover he was lieutenant of the County of Derby

5. And he came unto Derby, and said unto the Rulers thereof, and to the mighty men of the neighbouring villages, come unto me all ye that are loyal, and hearken unto my Voice.

6. For Issachar, the Pretender, is approaching; he hath taken the Capital of Caledonia, and threat-neth to bring us to Bondage, and to put a Yoke upon our Necks, and to cause us to bow down to Idols

7. Now, therefore, be ye steadfast and unmoveable; Gird every Man his Sword upon his Thigh, and let us behave ourselves valiantly, that George the King may know that the Men of Derby are good and true

8. Moreover he said unto them, unstring all your Purses, that we may raise a Regiment, and I will largely contribute thereto, my Son also shall lay on an helping Hand

9. And he began to collect; albeit many who had large Possessions were poor in Spirit; and the Sum collected amounted to six hundred Talents

10. And he began to appoint Captains over Tens, and Captains over Fifties, Lieutenants also, and Standard-Bearers appointed he

11. Moreover, at the Request of Nathan, were many appointed, not Men of Valour, serving only for Pay; and this grieved Devonshire sorely; for he said surely we shall become a Scorn and Derision unto our Enemies

12. And the Number of the Regiment was six hundred Men

13. And the Men were array'd in Blue, according to the Tradition of Samuel the Scribe; albeit it was a Colour of no Repute, for the Men of that Garb had fled before their Enemies in Germany

14. Now there was among the Captains a Man nam'd L w of the Tribe of H.....l...a, he was a mighty Hunter; and he said unto his Company, verily Issachar and his Men are Rebels, therefore we will pursue them unto the uttermost Corners of the Land, until we have destroy'd them; for he said in his Heart, they will flee before us, even as the timorous Hare fleeth

15. And he made great boasting among his Kinsfolk and Acquaintance, saying, my Company are all brave Men, they will follow me wheresoever I go

16. And Devonshire sent letters unto the several Officers, saying, gather yourselves together both you and your Men, that I may review you

17. So they assembled themselves and came to Derby, even as he had said unto them

18. And they drew out into a Place called the Holmes, the same is encompassed with the River Derwent, and were reviewed there

19. And Devonshire look'd, and behold many of them were Striplings, and not able to wield a Sword

20. And he shook his Head, and said, are these thy mighty Men O Derby! The Lord protect thee, for vain is the Help of these Men

21. And while they were yet in the Field, Tidings were brought saying, Issachar is at Ashbourn, and he will be with you on the morrow

22. And Devonshire heard all these Words; and his Wrath was kindled, and he said, surely their advanc'd Guard cannot exceed six hundred Men; why then should we be afraid? Let every man be of good Cheer, and prepare himself for Battle; let us meet them upon the Plains of Shirley, for I trust in the Lord that we shall discomfit them

23. Albeit Fear came upon them and Sorrow, so that they hearkened not to the Voice of Devonshire: For they said one to another, should we be slain, our Wives would grieve, and our damsels would make Lamentation

24. So every man took up his Weapons and prepared to flee

25. And when Devonshire saw that he prevailed not, he reasoned with them, saying, if you are determined to go home, let us join ourselves unto William the King's Son, who lieth in Staffordshire, or unto Wade the General, who is in the Province of York; peradventure we may serve our Country

26. And they communed amongst themselves, saying, if we join ourselves unto William we shall be in great Danger; but if we join ourselves unto Wade, then we shall be safe, for behold he is a peaceable Man

27. So they went forwards to Nottingham, under Covert of the Night; and Devonshire said go to refresh yourselves, lest you faint by the way, and lest ye be slain upon an empty stomach

28. And there was given to each Man a Portion of Bread and Cheese moreover they had strong Drink in Abundance

29. And about the tenth Hour they departed, some shouting as for Victory, others weeping and swearing and gnashing of Teeth; and the Cry of them was great

30. And they journeyed and came unto Borrows-Ash, a Village on the Way as thou goest to Nottingham: There they made War upon the Poultry, moreover they did eat plentifully, and drank much strong Drink, and departed forgetting to pay

31. And it came to pass as they drew nigh to Nottingham, that the Noise and Fame of them was heard, and it was told, saying, Issachar is coming, verily he is on this Side Stapleford, and the Men of Nottingham were sore afraid, and their hearts failed them

32. And they sent Messengers to Spy out the Road, and to bring them Intelligence

33. And the Messengers return'd unto them, saying, it is even as you have heard, for the young Man is coming; moreover his Army consists of ten thousand Men

34. And the Rulers thereof arose, and laid their Heads together, and they said one to another, lo! the young Man cometh for Money, let every Man prepare his Mite, and it shall be well with the Town, and he will be merciful to us, our Wives, and our Daughters

35. Albeit he came not, so the Money was otherwise employ'd

36. And Devonshire came unto Nottingham: And it came to pass when the Men of the Town, even the Men of Nottingham, saw that they had been afraid where there was no Danger, they threw up their Hats, saying, God bless King George, and may all the Machinations of Issachar come to Nought

37. Albeit Issachar was at Derby and heard them not

38. And when they had refreshed themselves, they looked one upon another, and said, this is no abiding Place for us, neither is there safety in Nottingham

39. And they journeyed Northwards towards Mansfield, by way of Sherwood, the same is the King's Forest

40. Now there was among them a Standard Bearer named M...lls of the Tribe of St Giles, he was a Man of War from his Youth, but a great Boaster, moreover he was a Publican and a Sinner

41. And he, vaunting himself, said, in the Days of my Youth I was accounted a Man of Valour, and when a drunken Blacksmith offended me, I smote him with the Edge of the Sword that he died, so will I do likewise unto Issachar, for what is he that defieth the Armies of George our King

42. And whilst they journeyed, there came a lying Messenger unto them, which said Issachar cometh with Speed, he will be with you in Half an Hour

43. And M'''lls cried out with a loud voice, saying, Halt ye Men in the Front, for our Rear is sorely press'd, and we shall inevitably be cut off

44. And they laugh'd him to scorn saying, how is the Mighty fallen, and his Honour laid in the Dust, nevertheless they slack'd not their Pace and happy was he that was swiftest of Foot

45. And they came safe unto Mansfield, and there abode that Day

46. And they sent out Parties to reconnoitre, lest they should be surpriz'd unawares

47. And they returned in the Night (having heard much talking, and a great Noise like unto the trampling of an Army) and they made their Report unto Devonshire, saying, now of a truth the Young Man approacheth, we are not deceived, for we have seem them with our Eyes, and their Van-Guard is about two thousand

48. And when the Men of Captain L W heard this, they cry'd out, saying, Captain what shall we do to be sav'd? And he answer'd them RUN, LADS, RUN, and he turned his Back, and fled, and they follow'd him

49. This was done that the words of the Captain might be fulfilled which he spoke unto Cope the Squire, saying, my men will follow me wherever I go

50. And they fled in great confusion, and many being assaulted with the Fumes of Liquor, and being sick with Fear spewed hideously; albeit it was a false alarm, for they were only an Herd of horned Cattle, which their Owners were driving to a place of Security

51. And one of these men lost, in his Flight, a war-like instrument, call'd a Drum, yet he turned not back to look after it

52. And Gr..tt.n, the Lieutenant, came riding furiously, and he whipp'd his Horse cruelly, saying, flee swiftly, for on they speed dependeth my Life

53. And saw not the Drum, but rose upon it and burst it; and the Noise thereof was like the Report of a Great Gun; and the Beast was in a Fright, and threw his Rider to the ground, and he roar'd terribly, crying, oh! I am slain! and the stench of this Man was grievous to be borne

54. And when they came to Redford they abode until Word was brought that the Young Man was return'd from Derby, by the Way which he came

55. And they returned back, and when they came nigh unto Derby, they gave great shouts, saying, hail Derby, happy are we to behold thee, for we greatly feared never to have seen thee again

56. And they came unto Derby with Joy and Gladness; albeit they were soon discharg'd, for Issachar had taken the Money which should have maintained them

57. So they were discharg'd, and each Man went his Way, some unto their Labours sore against their Wills, but others said we are Gent. neither will we do any more servile work, and these adhered to Granby the Marquess

58. Now the rest of the Acts of the Blues are they not well known, and the Money that was expended by them is it not written in the Book of Samuel the Scribe? And these Men are called the Drivers of Cattle even unto this very Day

Appendix 4

A Derby woman and her maid

This amusing jeu d'esprit was originally published in the Chester Journal, was reproduced as a broadside and was later printed in Chambers "History of the Rebellion". It is illustrative of the effect that Prince Charles' personal charm and charisma supposedly had on the female population of the towns which he passed through (see e.g. Beppy Bryom in Manchester).

Mistress - Jenny, come here: I'm told that you have been To see this man.
Jenny - What man?
Mistress - Why, you have seen
The young Pretender, hussy, at his lodging:
Is it not so? Come, tell me without dodging
Jenny - Why, really Madam, I was passing by
Thinking no harm- not in the least- not I
And somebody or other that I met -
Mistress - What somebody?
Jenny - Indeed I now forget
Said what a handsome man he was - and so,
Begging your pardon, Madam, I did go;
But had no ill intention in the thing;
A cat may look, as folks say, at a king
Mistress - King do you call him, ye rebellious slut?
Jenny - I did not call him so, good madam, but -
Mistress - But me! - no butting, not another day
Shall any rebel in my service stay:
I owe you twenty shillings - there's a guinea -
Pack up, and go about your business Jenny.
Matters are come, indeed, to a fine pass;
The next thing, I suppose, you'll go to mass
Jenny - To mass! What road? For I don't know the place,
Nor could I tell which way to turn my face
Mistress - Turn! - you'll turn papist, and believe black's white
Jenny - Why, bless me, madam, I han't lost my sight!
Mistress - And then the priest will bid you cut my throat.
Jenny - Dear loving mistress, how you talk by rote!
I would not hurt a hair of your dear head,

Were all the priests in mass to kill me dead;
And, I don't say it with design to brag,
Since I've been with you, you han't lost a rag.
I cut your throat! because I saw the Prince,
And never thought of black or white e'er since.
Mistress - Good! This is you that did not call him king!
And is not prince, ye minx, the self same thing?
Jenny - You are so hasty, madam, with your snarles;
Would you ha' me ca' the gentleman plain Ch--s?
Mistress - Prince Ch---s again! Speak out your treason tales
His Royal Highness, Ch--s, the Prince of W---s
Jenny - Oh! madam, you say more of him than me,
For I said nothing of his pedigree.
Mistress - Pedigree! Fool - what would the wench be at?
What pedigree has any bastard brat?
Jenny - Nay, I'm no herald: be he what he will,
He is a charming man to look at still;
When I was got in there amongst the throng,
His Royal Highness
Mistress - Hussy, hold your tongue
Jenny - You called him so yourself but just e'en now
Mistress - yes, so I did; but then the manner how?
Jenny - And will you turn a servant out o' doors
Because her manners be'n't so fine as yours?
Mistress - Jenny! I say you had no business neither
To see the creature, nor go near him either.
Jenny - Creature! - nay, pardon, madam, he is no creature
But a sweet comely Christian every feature.
Mistress - No creature! Would you worship him, you dunce?
Jenny - I would you were to see his worship once
Mistress - How can the girl cross-question like a fool?
Or think that I should go and see the tool?
Jenny, though you have done so far amiss,
I pity such an ignorance as this;
If you'll go mind your work as heretofore,
And keep at home, I'll pass the matter o'er.
Jenny - Ah, madam, you're so good, let me but speak
My simple mind, or else my heart will break;
I've such a strange foreboding in my heart,
If you but saw him once, we should not part.
Do see him once - what harm is there in seeing?

If, after that, there be not an agreeing,
Then call me twenty rebel sluts - if you
When you have seen him be'n't a rebel too.

Now whether Jenny did persuade her dame,
Has not, as yet, been trumpeted by fame;
Sometimes there happen to be secret views,
That are not put into the public news;
But by report that private rumour gives,
She'll never part with Jenny while she lives!

APPENDIX 5

A True Relation of the Behaviour, as well as the description, of such part of the Rebells which were quartered at the house of Wm. Bateman Town Clerk in Derby during their continuance there

Be it remembered that on Wednesday the 4th day of Decemr 1745 the Rebels marched from Ashbourne to Derby with their pretended Prince and his Adherents, the First Division or Vanguard of Horse came abt. 12 o'clock in the morning, and others continued coming in till about 8 at night with their Artillery; [they] were supposed to be about 6, or 7000d, tho they gave out that they were 9000d or more. They stayed till ffriday morning.

The delightful Complimt of them quartered on me by Billet, about six o'clock on Wednesday Evening, were 6 Officers (one a Major as they stiled him) 40 private Men, with 8 picked up Shabby Horses, some with't Saddles or Bridles, others with Halters, and pieces of Bridles and Ropes about their Heads and Necks, and poor Saddles or a Sort of Padds stuffed with straw upon them.

Most of these Men after their entrance into my House (I thot) looked like so many ffiends just turned out of Hell to ravage the Kingdom and cut throats, and, under their plaids nothing but a various sort of butchering weapons were to be seen. The sight at first must be thought (as it really was) very shocking and horrible. But these wretches being fatigued with their long March from Leek on Wednesday, soon after they came into my house, stuffed themselves well with Bread Cheese and Ale, and then about 20 of 'em before a great ffire in my Hall, order'd by them, call'd for a large quantity of Straw and nestled into it for Repose, and the Remaindr of them did the like in a large Laundry Room belonging to my House before two great ffires likewise order'd to be made there. The Officers took possession of my Parlour and Chambers they liked but, commanded what Supper and Liquor they would have, and expected me (tho in great pain with the Gout) my Wife and whole ffamily, to wait on them as if they were born so many petty princes, yet one of the Officers was tolerably civil and communicative, and really redressed some complaints made about the ill behaviour of his Men: My Hall after these Vagabond Creatures began to be warm, by such Numbers under the staw, and a great ffire near them, Stunk so of their itch and other nastinesses about them, as if they had been so many persons in a condemned Hole, and 'twill be very happy if they have left no contagion behind them. The next day (Thursday) the Officers and their Men grew more bold and insolent, order'd in an haughty tone, what meat and Drink they would have at their Meals, and if you was not at an instant ready to administer what they called for, some of them would surround you with fierce and savage Looks, as if they had been (in my comparison) so many Mutes appointed to strangle or some other way Assassin you. In this short time they eat me up near a side of Beef, 8 joints of Mutton, 4 Cheeses with abundance of white and brown Bread, particularly white, 3 couple of ffowls, and would have Drams continually as well as strong Beer Ale Tea etc. But what really did afford me some matter for an unavoidable laughter (tho my family in this miserable situation) was to see these Desperadoes, from Officers to common Men, at their several meals, first pull off their Bonnets, and then lift up their eyes in a most solemn manner, and mutter something to themselves, by way of saying Grace, as if they had been so many pure primitive Christians. As to their Dialect or language (from the idea I had of it) the same seem'd to be as if a herd of Hottentots, wild monkeys in a desert, or vagrant Gypsies had been jabbering screaming and howling together, and really this jargon of Speech was very properly suited to such a Sett of Banditti. I can't omit taking notice of another singular circumstance relating to these Gentry, and that is of the generous present they made me at Parting on Friday morning for the trouble and expense I was at, and the dangers undergone ('tho by the by I wished for no other compensation than the escape of my Family with their lives and of my House being plunder'd) which was a Regiment or two of Highland Lice, several loads of their filthy excrement, and other ejections of different colours, scattered before my Door, in the Garden, and elsewhere about my House, in the sight of all the Family, together with their wishes for a speedy Meeting again at Derby with their Prince crown'd with victory and peace. A true Portrait of those who would be our Rulers! But may God avert such an Event and grant that the English protestants (from the specimen so lately exhibited of the principles and schemes of these moroding and wandering Thieves) may soon hear of their utter extirpation. Anti-Pretender and Highlander (Dulce est pro patria Mori).

N.B. The religion of some of these common creatures (if they had any at all) seem'd to be a medley of Heathenism and popery, with a little tincture of the Scotch Kirk, but after all this complication of odd matter there did not appear the least Stricture of Humanity amongst them. So far I put in the Derby paper, wch, after got into the Magazine and the other Publick prints. In respect of the Treatment I rec'd, myself from others of these Miscreants not quarter'd at my House, twas in this manner. That when they had been a little settled in their Quarters on Wednesday Evening, a furious arm'd officer came to demand of me our County Subscription and Association, which I told him was never in my power to produce, so got rid of that Bully, then I hoped to hear no more from 'em in this mandatory way as to publick Matters. But the next day, after some thundering Rapps at my Door, came two other Officers, one seem'd a Scotch or ffrenchman, and the other a well dressed Englishman to demand of me my Horse, and in general to tell me there were several informations laid before their prince (which was the Appellation they distinguished him by) of my particular Disaffection towards him, and of being in conspiracy with several others to furnish the Duke of Devonshire with Horses, and that I must not only produce my own Horse secreted in or near the town as they were informed for the King and Duke's use, but give notice where others were to be met with, or else be instantly taken away prisoner. I told the Englishman (for the other was too outrageous to expostulate with) that four of my poor little Children were carried out of the town for Refuge, and my Horse used on that occasion, but where they were fled to, could not tell. Upon that he said the reason was a good one, and forc'd the other officer away with him. Soon after this an Hussar (as he called himself) came and took my Subscription Money, the one half had been paid before, and a short time after that, Another Rascal called for the same money again, and forced me to send a Man with him, to the other Officer who rec'd it. I was pretty afraid some Derby Incendiaries they had inlisted, or some others - Enemies to the Corporation, would have prompted these plunderers to have called for the Corporation Books, Charters and Burgesses Stamped Rolls in my custody for the destroying of the same, which would have brought great confusion to this Corporation and taken off all the legal Evidence (without otherwise remedied) for the support of a Borough Election, and so consequently have much affected the Duke of Devonshire's interest in questions of that kind, but these Evidences have luckily escaped, and my staying here, I may say without Vanity, was not a little contributory to it, but such another Trial would be intolerable. My Wife and I were not in Bed from Monday night till Friday, but constantly on the Watch to attend these Scoundrel Visitants, and to this case I can most truly and solemnly subscribe my Name and have every Article of it further veryfyed if Desired.

Wm Bateman - 19th May 1746

Appendix 6

A letter from Dr Mather at Kedleston Hall

This letter from Robert Mather, tutor to Assheton Curzon (Sir Nathaniel's younger son), written to the elder son (also Nathaniel) who was then attending Oxford, dated 9th December 1745 gives details of the Jacobite raid on Kedleston on the night of Thursday 5th December. It was first printed in *Notes and Queries* in 1869 and was re-printed in 1933 in Eardley -Simpson's "Derby and the Forty-Five".

Dear Mr Curzon,

I must refer you to Mr Dickins for an account of the rebels at Derby. All Wednesday and Thursday we were free from any of them here. (Many of the servants saw them march by Langley and Mackworth.) Lord George Murray would have had Pegge join'd them, but they got no more of him than his gloves, which one of the Highlanders oblig'd him to part with. On Thursday night, between 11 and 12, as I was going to bed, I heard a great rapping at the gate. "Who's there?" "King James's men", they answered. Down went I, and by that time they were got to the east gates. They said they must come in. I told them it was a late hour to make a visit. One (that I afterwards found was an officer) spoke more civilly than the rest, and said that he must come in and speak with Sir N. I told him He was abed. He said He must see him. I told him what commands he had to Sir N, I wou'd carry. And so bid the servants to open the Gates, and show'd them into the Servants' Hall. There were about 6 or 7 Highlanders arm'd in the Hussar Fashion, each with a brace of pistols in their hands, and a brace in their girdles, a broad sword, and one or two of them had a musket slung on his shoulder. That rascal Hewit, Bro. to the man yt mends the roads, was with them, and I believe was the man that brought them hither. He had listed with them at Derby. The officer went with me into the Steward's room, and told me his business with Sir N was to desire He wou'd furnish them with some horses; that he was inform'd He might get 9 or 10 good ones there, but half the number or less wou'd content him; that he would take none but what Sir N cou'd spare, none that he kept for his own riding, &c. He made apologies for the late hour, and said, rather than disturb my Lady (who I told him was ill) He wou'd go away without waiting to have his request comply'd with. He was extremely civil, and when I asked him whether that was ye full of his Commands to Sir N, He added that if Sir

N cou'd spare him a brace or two of good Pistols, He shou'd be oblig'd to him. (By this time the rest had gone down, and were sharing the Pistols in the Servants' Hall). I deliver'd his message to Sir N. No other answer cou'd be given to armed men, than that the groom shou'd show them what Horses were in the Stable, and they must take what they wanted. They were disappointed of their expectation when they saw the contents of the stables. You will guess how the stables were furnish'd when I tell you what they took, viz, the two old brown mares, Miss Glanville, and out of the Coach Horse Stable, Old Bully. (there were a set left in the latter, 'tho the best of them were put out of the way and others put in their stead, as was done with the rest, expecting a visit.) They went away with these saddled and bridled, and the Pistols, and that was all. They wou'd drink very little, and gave so little disturbance that my Lady and half the family knew not of their having been in the House till Morning. They were poor men by way of Soldiers. Your Brother came down, and looking upon them thro' the window in the Servants' Hall, one of them said He wou'd shoot him thro' the Head. Another said 'You Villain, I'll shoot you if you don't hold your tongue.' The officer told me they expected an action before they got to Leicester. He was very courteous to your Brother. they gave Anthony and Tom the Helper Shillings, and went away. They got Horses from most Houses about Derby in the same way. Ex Turner happened to be coming from Radbourne Common that way as they were marching by Langley. He had a race with some of them to save his mare, and one of them fir'd to bring him to, but He had the heels of them. He believes it was only Powder, for he knows a bullet He says by the wheezing. They listed Sparks, the fishing tackle man at Derby, but sent him back from Ashburn as too great a rogue to keep with them. He fell to plundering at Bradley, so He will probably be hang'd. The Chevalier, Duke of Perth and other officers of the Guards, were at Ld Exeter's House, Ld George Murray ay Mr Heathcote's. Ld and Lady Ogilvie and Mr and Mrs Murray at Mr Francis's. When they march'd out of Derby, Miss Glanville was seen dancing among them with a Highlander on her back. 'Oh!' crys he; 'this will gollope, gollope, this will gollope!' Lady Curzon was out of order last week, but is better. Blessings Love and Services to you in abundance. Sir N. bids me tell you, whenever you will give him a day's notice, you shall have the Horses sent to Oxford, or the Coach to meet you at Northampton, wch you will. Service to Nat Lister. He must come with you.

I am, dear Mr Curzon,
Yours affectly,
Ro Mather

Appendix 7

List of Subscribers to the Declaration at Derby
28th September 1745

WHEREAS, a most wicked and unnatural Rebellion is begun in that part of Great Britain called Scotland, by the eldest Son of the Pretender, against our rightful Sovereign King George, in order to subvert our Religion and Liberties, and to entail Popery and Slavery on us and on our Posterity: We his Majesty's most Loyal Subjects, whose names are hereunto subscribed, do hereby declare, our utmost abhorrence of so wicked an attempt; and in the most solemn manner engage, that we will, at the hazard of our Lives and Fortune, Support, and defend our excellent Constitution in Church and State, and oppose all attempts against his Majesty's Person and Government, particularly the Rebellion now carried on in favour of a Popish abjur'd Pretender. And we hereby promise and engage to meet together from time to time to concert and execute such measures as may be necessary for effecting the purposes of this our Association.

Devonshire	Hartington	Sir Nathaniel Curzon
Sir Thomas Abney	Sir Woollaston Dixie	Robert Coke
George Venables Vernon	Littleton Poyntz Meynell	Sir John Statham
Sir Robert Burdett	Sir Henry Harpur	William Cotton
James Shuttleworth	German Pole	Samuel Sanders
Bache Thornhill	Joseph Offley	William Fitzherbert
Leake Okeover	John Gilbert Cooper	Rowland Morewood
Edward Mundy	Henry Coape	John Rotherham
Chambers Bate	Rowe Port	Brook Boothby
Henry Bourne	Robert Wilmot	Joh. Gisborne
Christopher Orton	Edward Wilson	Richard Harpur
Samuel Crompton Jun	John Addenbrooke	John Griffith
John Stone	John Simpson	Jonathan Peake
Richard Wilmot DD	Clement Rosington	Matthew Pilkington
Robert Newton	John Taylor	Lucas Spilsbury
James Gisborne	Henry Mainwaring	Thomas Beighton
Thomas Borrow	William Asteley	John Mark Morgan
William Hope MD	Obadiah Bourne	James Gisborne Jun
Samuel Bristow	Thomas Barker	Henry Every
Hugh Bateman	Samuel Burton	William Bagshaw
Nathaniel Hurd	William Hunter	John Hope
John Flamstead	William Newton	John Gisborne Jun
John Clayton	Nicholas Twigg	John Wall
Hugh Bateman Jun	Samuel Heathcote	Nicholas Thornhill

Robert Holden
Humphrey Booth
Strelley Pegge
Richard Bagshaw
Robert Dale
John Rotton
Thomas White
Exuperius Turner
Henry Peach
John Rolaston
Philip Gell
William Alsop
Richard Bateman
Samuel Crompton
William Roberts
Gilbert Rhodes
John Longden
Henry Peter Lanolel
Richard Whitby
Robert Greensmith
William Bateman
Richard Clayton
John Bayley
Goodere Fletcher
John Edwards
Samuel Fox
Charles Hurt
Eardley Wilmot
Edward Goodwin
Samuel Cooper
Gilbert Icox
Thomas Holland
Benjamin Taylor
Thomas Leecroft

Chaworth Hallows
Joshua Smith
Richard Pyott
Thomas Chetham
William Locket
George Brentnall
Wm Hodgkinson
John Wood
John Hieron
James Brough
Thomas Shipton
Benjamin Blyth
Robert Fletcher
Benjamin Granger
Richard Milnes
Thomas Gisborne
William Clarke
Benjamin Clive
Sampson Copestake
Joseph Hayne
Robert Wood
Thomas Fisher
Linley Simpson
Thomas Boultbee
Richard Milnes
Edward Wilmot
John Pickering
Thomas Boufoy
Lawrence Bourne
William Evans
Joseph Bateman Jun
Thomas Harris
Ferdinando Lowe

Thomas Seaward
Thomas Docksey
Leonard Fosbrook
John Fitzherbert
William Bagshaw
Thomas Chambers
Henry Fletcher
John Holland
Francis Barber
William Daniel
George Pascall
Thomas Everard
Anthony Tissington
Brabason Hallows
Henry Green
Thomas Bennet
William Osbourne
John Morton
William Turner
John Wilkinson
Samuel Pole
Joseph James
Joshua Winter
Francis Rivett
William Brookes
Gilbert Cheshire
Henry Eyre
William Bowyer
Edward Lowe
Henry Clutton
Thos Beard - *Clerk*
John Town - *Clerk*
R Heathcote – *Clerk*

N B That several of the Gentlemen and Clergy of distant parts of the County, from DERBY, meet at *Chesterfield* on *Monday* next, being the last day of this month, to sign this Association. And several others being ill, or absent, the same will be conveyed to them for that purpose.

Note also. That another meeting of the Lord Lieutenant, Gentlemen, and Clergy, is appointed to be at the *King's Head* in *Derby*, on *Thursday* next, being the 3rd of *October*.

Each Petty Constable is to give immediate notice of the next meeting at *Derby*, to all Gentlemen and Clergy within their respective districts.

JOSEPH HAYNE *Clerk of the Peace*

Appendix 8

A list of the Subscribers in Derby [to the Derbyshire Blues Regiment] who paid all or part of their subscription money to the Rebell Collector

Mr Hugh Bateman for himself & son	60. 0. 0
Borrow, the Recorder	30. 0. 0
Mr Wm Bateman	2. 2. 0
Mr Jos Bateman	2. 2. 0
Mr Bainbrigge	10. 0. 0
Mr Bennett in part of £5.5.0. subscribed pd [sic]	2.12.6
Mr Crompton in pt of 100 subscribed only	10. 0.0
Mr Crompton Jnr	20. 0.0
Mr Cheshire	10. 0.0
Mr Chambers	10. 0.0
Mr Eyre	50. 0.0
Mr Tof (?)	25. 0.0
Mr Franceys in pt of £10.10 pd	5. 5.0.
Mr Fowler	2. 2.0
Mr Thos Gisborne	50. 0.0
Dr Hope in pt of £6.6.0 only	2. 2.0
Mr John Hope	2. 2.0
The Mayor of Derby	2. 2.0
Mr Hayne	2. 2.0
Mr Lockett	3. 3.0
Mr Lowe	4. 4.0
Mr Mellor	4. 4.0
Mr Peach	5. 5.0
Mr Roberts	5. 5.0
Mr Thos Rivett	21. 0.0
Mr Smith	5. 5.0
Mr Turner	20. 0.0
Mr Winter	3. 3.0
Mr Richd Wright	2. 2.0
Mr Thos Chambers	3. 3.0
Derby Corporation in pt of £40 only pd £37	37. 0.0.
Mr Wm Storer	5. 5.0

	428.12.6
Pd by Mr Heathcote the Ballance in his hands of the Subscription Money	
	18. 0.0
Levyed by Excise	**665. 0.0**
TOTAL	**1111.12.6**

Appendix 9

Some memorials of the Jacobite invasion in and around Derby

ASHBOURNE

Ashbourne Hall, Cockayne Avenue - part of this hall, where Prince Charles stayed on 3rd December 1745, remains and is now self-catering accommodation. There is also an information board with details of the Jacobite invasion of Derbyshire adjacent to the free bus stop on the new trading estate just off the A515, and a Blue Plaque outside the Town Hall.

DERBY

The Cathedral Church of All Saints - a plaque at the end of the right had aisle, just before the Chancel, commemorates the service held by the Jacobites on Thursday 5th December 1745

The Bonnie Prince Charlie Statue - this, the only statue of Prince Charles Edward Stuart in Britain, stands on the site of Exeter House, behind the Cathedral Chapter House on Full Street, which was the Prince's headquarters. Cast in bronze by sculptor Anthony Stones, it was unveiled in 1995 to commemorate the 250th anniversary of the Prince's arrival in Derby. Its erection owes much to the efforts of local historian Richard Felix, a founder member of the Prince Charles Edward Stuart Society which annually commemorates the Jacobite occupation of the city with a re-enactment of the event at Swarkestone Bridge. Exeter House would have stood between the statue and the River Derwent.

The Convent of the Sisters of Mercy, Bridge Gate - this Catholic convent, standing next to the Catholic church of St Mary's (the first Catholic church to be built in England after the Reformation, and dating back to 1836), was formerly the home of Alderman Thomas Gisborne. It was occupied byWilliam Murray, Marquis of Tullibardine, the elder brother of Lord George Murray, and titular Duke of Atholl in the Jacobite peerage.

Lloyds Bank (formerly Bingham's House) on the corner of Irongate and Sadler Gate - much altered over the years, this was the billet of John Murray, Earl of Nairne, a cousin of Lord George Murray and commander of the Jacobite regiment that bore his name.

Franceys' House, 3 Market Place - this Grade II listed mansion built in 1694, now includes the "Walkabout" pub. In December 1745 it was the quarters of some of the wives of the senior Jacobite commanders, including Lady Murray of Broughton (wife of the Prince's secretary, who later turned King's evidence) and Lady Ogilvy

Mr Jorrocks pub, Irongate - Originally erected in 1693, in 1745 this was "The George Inn" where the first meeting to raise money for the Derbyshire Blues was held. A blue plaque commemorates the event.

Jacobean House, The Wardwick - this is one of two town houses which, in 1745, were owned by Alderman Samuel Heathcote. He was host to Lord George Murray and his entourage, but it is unclear whether their quarters were here or at Heathcote's other house on Tenant Street which was demolished many years ago. It is likely that they were at Tenant Street, because that was adjacent to the Prince's quarters at Exeter House. However, there is little doubt that Jacobean House was occupied by senior officers in the Jacobite army - sadly we do not know for certain who they were.

Meynell's House, 22-24 Irongate, opposite the Cathedral - this very early (by Derby standards) house was constructed about 1660 and was occupied by the Jacobite cavalry commander Lord Pitsligo and his entourage

Derby Museum, The Strand - there is a "Bonnie Prince Charlie Room" at Derby Museum. This is furnished with panelling rescued from Exeter House when it was demolished in 1854 and contains a number of exhibits relating to the Rising including Jacobite medals and the ring given to the mother of Bonnie Prince Charlie's food taster.

Otherwise, Derby is not well provided with buildings from the mid-eighteenth century and earlier, largely due to the ravages inflicted on the city by the local planning department over many years, particularly since the construction of the ring road which commenced in the mid 1960's. However, there are a number of additional buildings still extant which were there at the time of the Jacobite occupation. Although we cannot associate them with any named Jacobites, there is no doubt that they were patronised by the Jacobite troops. Notable amongst them are the Dolphin Inn, a short walk from the Cathedral, dating from 1529 (and thus Derby's oldest existing public house), and the Old Bell Inn on Sadler Gate, Derby's only remaining coaching inn and currently undergoing extensive renovation. The Jacobite troops marched past it on their way into Derby and we can be certain that many of them drank there (whether "at free quarters" the writer is unable to say!)

KEDLESTON

Kedleston Hall, now owned by the National Trust, is not the original hall visited by the Jacobites (see letter from Dr Mather at Appendix 8), but was built to replace the earlier residence. However, it does contain one very interesting relic, namely one of the mortars brought to Derby as part of the Jacobite artillery train and abandoned by them on the retreat.

SWARKESTONE

Swarkestone Bridge - the causeway to the bridge from the south is the same one that was extant when the bridge was seized by the Jacobite rearguard. There is an information board adjacent which gives details.

The Crewe and Harpur Pub - in the beer garden there is a cairn and bronze plaque to commemorate the seizure of the bridge and the fact that this was as far south as the Jacobite army reached.

Appendix 10

The Jacobite Rose (see illustration 23)

This curious memorial to the Jacobites who were executed for their part in the '45 was engraved and printed by Sir Robert Strange. In 1745, he fell in love with the daughter of a strongly Jacobite family, Isabella Lumsden, while he was making his way as a young engraver in Edinburgh and at her behest joined the Jacobite army and marched with it to Derby as a trooper in Elcho's troop of the Prince's Lifeguards. He designed the plates for producing a paper currency for the Prince and was engaged on this task in Inverness when the Battle of Culloden was fought. Subsequently he managed to escape and in due course he married Isabella and they enjoyed a long and happy life together. Robert eventually became a prominent and esteemed society artist. He executed this engraving many years after the event, and it is believed that there were two of them. I think that this is the first time that the names on the engraving have been fully identified and details are appended below. Several of the names will be familiar to readers of this book as members of the Jacobite army that marched to Derby. Fourteen of them were officers, sergeants or privates in the Manchester Regiment who had been taken prisoner at Carlisle when it was re-captured by the Duke of Cumberland on 20th December 1745.

BOTTOM PETAL

James Harvie - Linlithgow. Quartermaster in Kilmarnock's Regiment. Executed on 28th October 1746

Edward Clavering - Private from Northumberland in the Manchester Regiment. Executed on 1st November 1746

Benjamin Mason - Irish weaver. Sergeant in Gordon of Glenbucket's Regiment. Executed on 1st November 1746

Charles Gordon - Of Terpesie. Volunteer in Gordon of Glenbucket's Regiment. executed on 15th November 1746 aged 60

D Frazier - Possibly Daniel Fraser, a deserter from Loudon's Regiment. Executed on 1st November 1746

Donald Macdonald - Probably Donald MacDonald of Tirnadris, a Major in MacDonald of Keppoch's Regiment captured after the battle of Falkirk. Executed on 18th October 1746

BOTTOM RIGHT PETAL

Edward Roper - Lancashire Weaver. Private in the Manchester Regiment. Executed on 18th October 1746

James Brand - Edinburgh watchmaker & Major in Bagot's Hussars. Executed on 18th October 1746

?Horn - Unidentified. No person of that name was executed for his part in the Rising, nor can I trace his name under the muster rolls of any of the regiments involved. It could refer to Captain David Home of Duns, an officer in Balmerino's Horse executed on 28th October 1746

Rev Robert Lyon - Chaplain to the Forfarshire Regiment (Ogilvy's). Executed on 28th October 1746

Philip Hunt - Barber from Wigan. Sergeant in the Manchester regiment. Executed on 28th October 1746

Walter Ogilvie(y) - Writer [i.e. lawyer] from Banff. Lieutenant in the Duke of Perth's Regiment. Executed on 22nd August 1746

Valentine Holt - Clothworker (?from Manchester). Sergeant in the Manchester Regiment. Executed on 28th October 1746

Andrew Swan - Shoemaker, Edinburgh. Sergeant in the Manchester Regiment. Executed on 28th October 1746

James Nicolson - Coffee House Keeper. Lieutenant in Duke of Perth's Horse. Executed 2nd August 1746

William Hunter - Newcastle. Private in the Manchester Regiment. Executed 8th November 1746

David Row (or Roe) - Customs Officer from Anstruther. Volunteer in MacDonnell of Glengarry's Regiment. Executed on 8th November 1746

BOTTOM LEFT PETAL

Hugh Cameron - From Loch Arlaig. Officer in Cameron of Lochiel's Regiment. Executed 18th October 1746

James Innes - Overseer of Roads. Lt Colonel in Forfarshire Regiment (Ogilvy's). Executed 21st October 1746

Michael Dellard - Woolworker from Manchester. Private in the Manchester Regiment. Executed 21st October 1746

John Rowbocham - From Lancashire. Sergeant in the Manchester regiment. Executed 28th October 1746

John MacNaughton - Watchmaker from Edinburgh. Quartermaster in the Perthshire Horse (Strathallan's). Executed 18th October 1746

J Henderson of Castlemains - Writer (i.e. lawyer) from Lochmaben. Executed 21st October 1746

TOP RIGHT PETAL

John Wallace - Miller from Linthlithgow. Executed 15th November 1746
Robert Reid - Executed at Carlisle 15th November 1746
Michael Eaton - Weaver from Lancashire. Private in the Manchester Regiment. Executed 15th November 1746
Thomas Hayes - Lancashire. Private in the Manchester Regiment. Executed 15th November 1746
Barnabas Matthew - Lancashire. Private in the Manchester Regiment. Executed 15th November 1746
James Mitchell - Arnhall, Aberdeenshire. Private in Lord Lewis Gordon's Regiment. executed 15th November 1746

TOP LEFT PETAL

?David M Daniel - Unidentified. There is no-one of this name in the list of prisoners executed after the Rising
Donald MacDonald - Captain in MacDonald of Keppoch's Regiment and nephew of the clan chief. Executed 22nd August 1746
Andrew Wood - Shoemaker from Glasgow. Captain in John Roy Stuart's Edinburgh Regiment. Executed 28th November 1746
?Gordon - This could be either Alexander Gordon of Leith, a Captain in Gordon of Glenbucket's Regiment, executed on 28th November 1746, or Charles Gordon of Strathbogie, a Lieutenant in the same regiment, executed on 1st November 1746
Alexander Leith - From Collithy. A Captain in Gordon of Glenbucket's Regiment. Executed 28th November 1746
George Hamilton - From Redhouse. A Captain in Bagot's Hussars. Executed 1st November 1746

CENTRE PETALS

Francis Buchanan of Arnprior - From Leny House, Callander. Executed 19th October 1746
Sir Archibald Primrose - Of Dunipace. Captain in Bagot's Hussars. Executed 15th November 1746
John Hamilton of Sandstoun - Governor of Carlisle. Executed 15th November 1746
Francis Townley - Of Preston. Colonel of the Manchester Regiment. Executed 30th July 1746
David Morgan - Barrister of Monmouth. Captain in the Manchester Regiment. Executed 30th July 1746

EDGE

Charles Edward Stuart Born December 20th 1720
Henry Benedict Stuart Born February 23rd 1725

CENTRE

Martyred for King and Country 1746

Notes and references

Abbreviations

DANHSJ - Derbyshire Archaeological and Natural History Society Journal
DLSL - Derby Local Studies Library
DRS - Derbyshire Record Society
JRLS - Journal of Regional and Local Studies
JSAHR - Journal of the Society for Army Historical Research

Chapter 1

[1] For the background to the Jacobite movement and the history of the risings see in particular Christopher Duffy "*The '45*" London 2003 pages 32 to 47, and Sir Charles Petrie "*The Jacobite Movement*", London 1958

Chapter 2

[2] For the Prince's early life see Fitzroy MacLean "*Bonnie Prince Charlie*", London 1988 pages 3 - 21
[3] A G Murray MacGregor "*A Royalist Family Irish and French and Prince Charles Edward*" Edinburgh 1904 page 19 quoted in Charles Sanford Terry "*The Forty-Five*" Cambridge 1922 page 20
[4] The Journal of Aeneas Macdonald in Rev Robert Forbes "*The Lyon in Mourning*" Volume I , Edinburgh 1895 page 288 quoted in Terry op cit page 22
[5] George Lockhart "*The Lockhart Papers*" Volume II London 1817 page 479 quoted in Terry op cit page 25
[6] John Home "*The History of the Rebellion in the Year 1745*", London 1802 page 49 quoted in Terry op cit at page 31
[7] Robert Fitzroy Bell (Ed) "*Memorials of John Murray of Broughton*", Edinburgh 1898 page 194 quoted in Terry op cit at page 46
[8] A Francis Steuart (Ed) "*The Woodhouselee Manuscript*" London & Edinburgh 1907 page 25 quoted in Terry op cit pages 46 - 47
[9] Andrew Henderson "*The Edinburgh History of the Late Rebellion 1745 & 1746*" London 1752 page 24
[10] Chevalier Johnstone "*A Memoir of the Forty-Five*" London 1958 pages 36 - 37
[11] Henderson op cit pages 32" - 32

[12] The Duke of Perth quoted in Donald Nicholas "*The Young Adventurer*" London 1949 page 39

[13] David Lord Elcho "*A Short Account of the Affairs of Scotland in the Years 1744, 1745 and 1746*" Edinburgh 1907 quoted in Terry op cit at pages 61 - 62

[14] Bell op cit quoted in Terry op cit pages 63 - 64

Chapter 3

[15] Vanessa S Doe (Ed) "*The Diary of James Clegg of Chapel en le Frith 1708 - 1755*" Part 2 Volume III Derbyshire Record Society 1979 page 552

[16] Bell op cit quoted in Terry page 70

[17] *Daily Post* 12th December 1745 quoted in Duffy op cit page 247

[18] A H Tayler (Ed)"*The Narrative of John William O'Sullivan*" in "*1745 and After*" London 1938 page 96

[19] Johnstone op cit pages 54 - 56

[20] Walter Biggar Blaikie (Ed) "*A True Account of Mr John Daniel's Progress with Prince Charles Edward Stuart in the Years 1745 and 1746*" in "*The Origins of the Forty-Five*" Edinburgh 1916 page 115

[21] Elcho op cit quoted in Terry page 73

[22] Richard Parkinson (Ed) "*The Journal of Elizabeth Byrom in 1745*" Manchester 1857 pages 9 - 10

[23] Clegg op cit page 558

[24] Elcho op cit quoted in Terry op cit pages 73 - 74

[25] P J C Smith "*The Invasion of 1745 - the Drama in Lancashire and Cheshire*" Manchester 1993 page 33

[26] Rev Robert Forbes (Ed) "*Lord George Murray's Journal*" in "*Jacobite Memoirs of the Rebellion of 1745*" Edinburgh 1834 page 18 quoted in Terry op cit at page74

Chapter 4

[27] Daniel Defoe "*A Tour Through the Whole Island of Great Britain*" London 1986 page 460

[28] W Alfred Richardson "*Citizen's Derby*" London 1949 page 143

[29] Ibid pages 126 - 129

[30] Catherine Glover & Philip Riden (Eds) "*William Woolley's History of Derbyshire*" DRS Volume VI 1981 page 23

Chapter 5

[31] L Eardley-Simpson "*Derby and the Forty-Five*" London 1933 Appendix B at page 243

[32] Ibid page 14 quoting William Hutton "*History of Derby*" London 1791 page 243

Chapter 6

[33] Iain Gordon Brown & Hugh Cheape (Eds) "*Witness to Rebellion - John Maclean's Journal of the 'Forty-Five'*" Edinburgh 1996 page 27

[34] Eardley-Simpson op cit Appendix H at page 277

[35] Clegg op cit page 559

[36] *Gentleman's Magazine* Vol XV 1745 pages 708 - 710

[37] Eardley-Simpson op cit page 145

[38] Elcho op cit page 121

[39] F J McLynn "*The Jacobite Army in England*" Edinburgh 1983 page 25. See also the sketch of the Jacobite army prepared by Lord Elcho at illustration 3.

[40] For details of the dress and equipment of the Jacobite army see McLynn op cit Chapter 2 and Stuart Reid "*The Scottish Jacobite Army 1745 - 46*" London 2006

[41] Mrs (Katherine) Thomson "*Memoirs of the Jacobites of 1715 and 1745*" London 1845 Vol III page 279 quoted in Maxwell Craven "*The Derby Townhouse*" Derby 1987 page 120

[42] For details of the billeting arrangements in Derby generally see Maxwell Craven op cit.

[43] *Gentleman's Magazine* op cit

[44] Eardley-Simpson op cit pages 170 - 171

[45] Ibid page 171

[46] *Daily Post* 20th December 1745

[47] *Derby Mercury* 13th December 1745 page 3

[48] DLSL A.907.2MSS

[49] Mrs Katherine Thomson op cit pages 136 - 137

[50] "*The Prince's Household Book*" in Forbes op cit pages 100 - 101

[51] Eardley-Simpson op cit Appendix G at page 275

[52] Blaikie op cit pages 118 - 119

[53] Eardley-Simpson op cit Appendix H at page 276

[54] For details of the controversy surrounding the alleged celebration of a Catholic Mass at All Saints see Eardley-Simpson op cit pages 174 - 179

[55] Brown & Cheape op cit page 27

[56] James Ray "*A Compleat History of the Rebellion*" Bristol 1752 pages 156 - 157

[57] Eardley-Simpson op cit page 146

Chapter 7

[58] For details of the disposition of government forces see Duffy op cit pages 303 - 304 and Eardley-Simpson op cit Appendix I at pages 276 - 280

[59] Ibid

[60] Roy Hattersley - "*The Devonshires*" London 2013 page 193 et seq

[61] Ibid quoted on page 202 (Lord Charles Cavendish was in fact the uncle, not the brother, of the Marquis of Hartington)

[62] Clegg op cit page 552

[63] Eardley-Simpson op cit Appendix D at page 264

[64]John Beresford - "*Storm and Peace*" London 1936 page 27

[65] Ibid page 28

[66] Ibid page 34

[67] Ibid page 35

[68] Ibid page 23

[69] Ibid pages 40 - 41

[70] Clegg op cit page 558

[71] Beresford op cit page 56

Chapter 8

[72] Eardley-Simpson op cit page 143

[73] Ibid pages 143 - 144

[74] Ibid page 144

[75] DANHSJ Vol 89 (1969) pages 27 - 28

[76] G S Taylor (Ed) - "*The Life and Uncommon Adventures of Captain Dudley Bradstreet*" London nd page 127. For further information and discussion about the role of Bradstreet see also Rupert C Jarvis "*Collected Papers on the Jacobite Risings*" Vol II Manchester 1972 pages 94 - 106

[77] I owe this information to the generosity of Dr Eveline Cruickshanks in making available to me her unpublished research material on the role of Bradstreet which, to my mind, has decisively laid to rest his assertion that he was present at the Council of War

Chapter 9

[78] Home op cit page Appendix xxxii at page 156

[79] Forbes op cit "*Lord George Murray's Journal*" page 37

[80] The unpublished papers of Lord George Murray quoted in Katherine Tomasson "*The Jacobite General*" Edinburgh 1958 page 109

[81] Elcho op cit pages 124 - 125

[82] James Maxwell of Kirkconnel "*A Narrative of Charles Prince of Wales' Expedition to Scotland in the Year 1745*" Edinburgh 1861 page 28

[83] Robert Fitzroy Bell op cit page 239

[84] A H Tayler "*O'Sullivan's Narrative*" op cit page 102

[85] Rev J Charles Cox "*Three Centuries of Derbyshire Annals*" Derby 1890 Volume I pages 310 - 311

[86] Eardley-Simpson op cit page 123 et seq

[87] Lord George Murray "*Marches of the Highland Army*" in Forbes "*Jacobite Memoirs*" op cit page 39 quoted in Tomasson op cit pages 114 - 115

[88] A H Tayler "*O'Sullivan's Narrative*" op cit pages 102 - 103

[89] Elcho op cit page 340

[90] Quoted in Donald Nicholas "*The Young Adventurer*" London 1947 page 67

[91] Blaikie op cit page 119

Chapter 10

[92] Maxwell of Kirkconnel op cit page 78

[93] McLynn op cit page 139

[94] Eardley-Simpson op cit page 211

[95] Captain James Stuart "*The March of the Highland Army in the Years 1745 and 1746*" in "*The Spalding Club Miscellany*" Aberdeen 1841 Volume I page 303

[96] Home op cit page 156

[97] Forbes op cit page 47

[98] Tayler op cit page 103

[99] "*Gentleman's Magazine*" 1745 page 622

[100] Eardley-Simpson op cit Appendix J at page 280

[101] Blaikie op cit page 120

[102] Clegg op cit page 559

[103] Quoted in P J C Smith op cit page 38

[104] Ibid pages 39 - 40

[105] Parkinson op cit page 15

Chapter 11

[106] Johnstone op cit pages 86 - 87

[107] Robert Chambers "*History of the Rebellion of 1745 - 46*" Edinburgh 1869 page 241

[108] Johnstone op cit pages 122 - 124

[109] Livingstone, Aikman and Hart (Eds) "*No Quarter Given - The Muster Roll of Prince Charles Edward Stuart's Army 1745 - 46*" pages 225 - 9

[110] Clegg op cit page 582

Chapter 12

[111] Sir Charles Petrie in "*The Weekly Westminster*" 30th January 1926

[112] Eardley-Simpson op cit pages 229 - 230

[113] Petrie "*The Jacobite Movement*" op cit page 374

[114] Duffy op cit page 313

[115] Eardley-Simpson op cit page 105

[116] W S Lewis (Ed) "*Horace Walpole's Correspondence: Walpole to Mann 1742-45*" Volume 18 Yale 1955 page 169

[117] For details of the opposing forces and useful discussions of the strategic and tactical position of the Jacobite army and the government forces, Duffy op cit Chapter 11, Eardley-Simpson op cit Chapter VI and Jonathan Oates " *The Crisis of the Hanoverian State?*" in JSAHR LXXXI (2003) are all indispensable

Bibliography

The bibliography of books about Jacobitism and the Jacobite Rebellion of 1745 is enormous and would fill a sizeable volume on its own. This bibliography, therefore, has no pretentions to be definitive - it is merely a list of the books, articles and newspapers that I have consulted and found useful in the writing of this book. Many of the volumes listed have their own comprehensive bibliographies to which the reader is referred. For the abbreviations please refer to the introductory section of the footnotes.

Newspapers

Derby Mercury - November and December 1745
Gentleman's Magazine - November and December 1745
London Evening Post - December 1745
London Gazette - December 1745

Books

Bell Robert Fitzroy (Ed) - *Memorials of John Murray of Broughton* - Edinburgh - 1898

Beresford John - *Storm and Peace* - London - 1936

Blaikie Walter Biggar (Ed) - *The Origins of the Forty-Five and other Papers Relating to that Rising* - Edinburgh - 1916 (contains the Narrative of John Daniel and papers relating to John Murray of Broughton)

Brown Iain Gordon & Cheape Hugh (Eds) - *Witness to Rebellion - John Maclean's Journal of the Forty-Five* - Edinburgh - 1996

Butterton Harry - *Bonnie Prince & Burning Rebel* - Derby - 2011

Charteris Sir Evan (Ed) - *A Short Account of the Affairs of Scotland in the Years 1744, 1745 & 1746* - London - 1907 (contains the Narrative of David Lord Elcho)

Chambers Robert - *History of the Rebellion in Scotland 1745 & 1746* - Edinburgh - 1830

Cox Rev J Charles - *Three Centuries of Derbyshire Annals* - Derby - 1890

Craig Maggie - *Damn' Rebel Bitches - The Women of the '45* - Edinburgh - 1997

Craven Maxwell - *The Derby Townhouse* - Derby - 1987

Cruickshanks Eveline - *Political Untouchables - The Tories and the '45* - London - 1979

Doe V S (Ed) - *The Diary of James Clegg of Chapel-en-le Frith 1708-1755* - Derbyshire Record Society - 1978

Duffy Christopher - *The '45* - London - 2003

Eardley-Simpson L - *Derby and the Forty-Five* - London - 1933

Forbes Bishop Robert - *The Lyon in Mourning* - Edinburgh (3 Volumes) - 1895 (contains numerous letters, newspaper reports and the like)

Forbes Bishop Robert - *Jacobite Memoirs of the Rebellion of 1745* - Edinburgh 1841 (contains Lord George Murray's *Marches of the Highland Army* and *The Prince's Household Book*)

Gibson John S - *Ships of the '45* - London - 1967

Hattersley Roy - *The Devonshires* - London - 2013

Henderson Andrew - *The Edinburgh History of the late Rebellion* - London - 1752

Home John - *The History of the Rebellion in Scotland in the Year 1745* - London - 1822

Jarvis Rupert C - *Collected Papers on the Jacobite Risings - Volume I* - Manchester - 1971

Jarvis Rupert C - *Collected Papers on the Jacobite Risings - Volume II* - Manchester - 1972

Johnstone Chevalier de - *A Memoir of the Forty-Five* - London - 1958

Lang Andrew - *Prince Charles Edward* - Edinburgh - 1900

Lewis W S (Ed) - *Correspondence of Horace Walpole Volume 18* - Yale - 1955

Livingstone Alexander, Aikman Christian W H & Hart Betty Stuart (Eds) - *No Quarter Given - the Muster Roll of Charles Edward Stuart's Army 1745-46* - Glasgow - 2001

MacLean Fitzroy - *Bonnie Prince Charlie* - London - 1988

Macquoid G S - *Jacobite Songs and Ballads* - London - nd

Maxwell of Kirconnel James - *Narrative of Charles Prince of Wales Expedition to Scotland in the Year 1745* - Aberdeen - 1841

McLynn F J - *The Jacobite Army in England 1745* - Edinburgh - 1983

Monod Paul Kleber - *Jacobitism and the English People 1688-1788* - Cambridge - 1993

Nicholas Donald - *The Young Adventurer* - London - 1949

Oates Jonathan D - *The Jacobite Invasion of 1745 in North West England* - Lancaster - 2006

Petrie Sir Charles - *The Jacobite Movement* - London - 1959

Prebble John - *Culloden* - London - 1961

Ray James - *A Compleat history of the Rebellion... in the year 1745* - Bristol - 1752

Reid Stuart - *The Scottish Jacobite Army 1745-46* - London - 2006

Richardson W Alfred - *Citizen's Derby* - London - 1949

Seton Sir Bruce Gordon & Arnot Jean Gordon - *Prisoners of the '45* - Edinburgh - 1928

Smith Peter J C - *The Invasion of 1745 - The Drama in Lancashire & Cheshire* - Manchester - 1993

Stuart James - *The March of the Highland Army* - Spalding Club Miscellany Volume I -Aberdeen 1841

Tayler Alistair & Tayler Henrietta - *1745 and After* - London - 1938 (contains the *Narrative of John William O'Sullivan*)

Taylor G S (Ed) - *The Life and Uncommon Adventures of Captain Dudley Bradstreet* - London - nd c1930

Terry Charles Sanford - *The Forty-Five - A Narrative of the Last Jacobite Rising* - Cambridge - 1922

Tomasson Katherine - *The Jacobite General* - Edinburgh - 1958

Articles

Annand A McK - *The Life Guards of Prince Charles Edward 1745-6* - JSAHR LXXIII (1995)

Chambers R E E - *The Pole Family and the Forty-Five* - DANHSJ Volume 55- 1934

Eardley- Simpson Major L - *Radbourne & the Forty-Five* - DANHSJ Volume 36 - 1935

Leslie Major J H - *An Account of the Behaviour of the Derbyshire Regiment raised against the Rebels in the year 1745 under the command of His Grace the Duke of Devonshire* - DANHSJ Volume 22 - 1900

McLynn F J - *The Regional Distribution of Jacobite Support in England Before 1745* - JRLS (iii) 1984

Oates Jonathan D - *The Crisis of the Hanoverian State?* - JSAHR LXXXI (2003)

Potter G R - *A Government Spy in Derbyshire During the Forty-Five* - DANHSJ Volume 89 – 1969

INDEX

Page number in *italics* refer to figures. Please see the note on page 12 regarding spelling and names.

Lightning Source UK Ltd.
Milton Keynes UK
UKOW07f0829151115

262705UK00003B/17/P